OPPOSING
VIEWPOINTS®
SERIES

Cars in America

Other Books of Related Interest:

Opposing Viewpoints Series
Alcohol
America in the Twenty-First Century
American Values
Conserving the Environment
Energy Alternatives
Global Resources
Obesity
Oil
Popular Culture

Current Controversies Series
Alternative Energy Sources
Conserving the Environment
Pollution
Teens and Alcohol

At Issue Series
Drunk Driving
Foreign Oil Dependence
Is America's Culture in Decline?
What Sources of Energy Should Be Pursued?

"Congress shall make no law . . . abridging the freedom of speech, or of the press."

First Amendment to the U.S. Constitution

The basic foundation of our democracy is the First Amendment guarantee of freedom of expression. The Opposing Viewpoints Series is dedicated to the concept of this basic freedom and the idea that it is more important to practice it than to enshrine it.

OPPOSING VIEWPOINTS® SERIES

Cars in America

Andrea C. Nakaya, Book Editor

GREENHAVEN PRESS

An imprint of Thomson Gale, a part of The Thomson Corporation

THOMSON

™

GALE

Detroit • New York • San Francisco • San Diego • New Haven, Conn.
Waterville, Maine • London • Munich

Bonnie Szumski, *Publisher*
Helen Cothran, *Managing Editor*

For more information, contact:
Greenhaven Press
27500 Drake Rd.
Farmington Hills, MI 48331-3535
Or you can visit our Internet site at http://www.gale.com

LIBRARY OF CONGRESS CATALOGING-IN-PUBLICATION DATA

Cars in America / Andrea C. Nakaya, book editor.
    p. cm. -- (Opposing viewpoints)
  Includes bibliographical references and index.
  0-7377-3307-1 (lib. : alk. paper) 0-7377-3308-X
  1. Automobiles--United States. 2. Automobiles--Social aspects--United States.
3. Automobile driving--Social aspects--United States. 4. Transportation--United
States. I. Nakaya, Andrea C., 1976– II. Opposing viewpoints series (Unnumbered)
  TL23.C3655 2006
  303.48'32--dc22
                                                                2006041077

Printed in the United States of America
10 9 8 7 6 5 4 3 2 1

Contents

Chapter 3: How Should Youth Driving Be Regulated?

Chapter 4: How Can the United States Meet Its Future Transportation Needs?

Why Consider Opposing Viewpoints?

> *"The only way in which a human being can make some approach to knowing the whole of a subject is by hearing what can be said about it by persons of every variety of opinion and studying all modes in which it can be looked at by every character of mind. No wise man ever acquired his wisdom in any mode but this."*
>
> John Stuart Mill

In our media-intensive culture it is not difficult to find differing opinions. Thousands of newspapers and magazines and dozens of radio and television talk shows resound with differing points of view. The difficulty lies in deciding which opinion to agree with and which "experts" seem the most credible. The more inundated we become with differing opinions and claims, the more essential it is to hone critical reading and thinking skills to evaluate these ideas. Opposing Viewpoints books address this problem directly by presenting stimulating debates that can be used to enhance and teach these skills. The varied opinions contained in each book examine many different aspects of a single issue. While examining these conveniently edited opposing views, readers can develop critical thinking skills such as the ability to compare and contrast authors' credibility, facts, argumentation styles, use of persuasive techniques, and other stylistic tools. In short, the Opposing Viewpoints Series is an ideal way to attain the higher-level thinking and reading skills so essential in a culture of diverse and contradictory opinions.

In addition to providing a tool for critical thinking, Opposing Viewpoints books challenge readers to question their own strongly held opinions and assumptions. Most people form their opinions on the basis of upbringing, peer pressure, and personal, cultural, or professional bias. By reading carefully balanced opposing views, readers must directly confront new ideas as well as the opinions of those with whom they disagree. This is not to simplistically argue that everyone who reads opposing views will—or should—change his or her opinion. Instead, the series enhances readers' understanding of their own views by encouraging confrontation with opposing ideas. Careful examination of others' views can lead to the readers' understanding of the logical inconsistencies in their own opinions, perspective on why they hold an opinion, and the consideration of the possibility that their opinion requires further evaluation.

Evaluating Other Opinions

To ensure that this type of examination occurs, Opposing Viewpoints books present all types of opinions. Prominent spokespeople on different sides of each issue as well as well-known professionals from many disciplines challenge the reader. An additional goal of the series is to provide a forum for other, less known, or even unpopular viewpoints. The opinion of an ordinary person who has had to make the decision to cut off life support from a terminally ill relative, for example, may be just as valuable and provide just as much insight as a medical ethicist's professional opinion. The editors have two additional purposes in including these less known views. One, the editors encourage readers to respect others' opinions—even when not enhanced by professional credibility. It is only by reading or listening to and objectively evaluating others' ideas that one can determine whether they are worthy of consideration. Two, the inclusion of such viewpoints encourages the important critical thinking skill of objectively evaluating an author's credentials and bias. This evaluation will illuminate an author's reasons for taking a particular stance on an issue and will aid in readers' evaluation of the author's ideas.

It is our hope that these books will give readers a deeper understanding of the issues debated and an appreciation of the complexity of even seemingly simple issues when good and honest people disagree. This awareness is particularly important in a democratic society such as ours in which people enter into public debate to determine the common good. Those with whom one disagrees should not be regarded as enemies but rather as people whose views deserve careful examination and may shed light on one's own.

Thomas Jefferson once said that "difference of opinion leads to inquiry, and inquiry to truth." Jefferson, a broadly educated man, argued that "if a nation expects to be ignorant and free . . . it expects what never was and never will be." As individuals and as a nation, it is imperative that we consider the opinions of others and examine them with skill and discernment. The Opposing Viewpoints Series is intended to help readers achieve this goal.

David L. Bender and Bruno Leone,
Founders

Introduction

"We have staked our entire way of life on a non-renewable resource that may be largely exhausted in our lifetime."

—www.hybridcars.com

Ever since mass production of the automobile began in the United States in the early 1900s, the country has led the world in car ownership. According to UN statistics, America has more motor vehicles per person than any other country. Cars have become an essential part of life for most Americans, and the majority of these vehicles are fueled by gasoline, which is made from oil. Unfortunately, there is an increasing realization that America's dependence on cars fueled by oil cannot last forever. Indeed, there are fears that world oil supplies are beginning to run out, and that because America is dependent on foreign oil imports, its supply of this crucial energy source is vulnerable to disruption. Because of the popularity of cars, any change in America's ability to obtain affordable oil will have an enormous impact on society.

In recent years there has been increasing concern over how long the world's oil supplies will last. As energy investment banker Matthew Simmons explains, "Oil and gas resources are basically nonrenewable and so someday they will basically run out." According to the widely cited Hubbert peak theory, introduced by American geophysicist M. King Hubbert in 1956, there will eventually be a peak in world oil production, followed by declining production. Many people believe that peak is imminent. For example, energy experts James Jordan and James R. Powell assert, "Oil experts agree that Hubbert's Peak is inevitable. . . . The only uncertainty is when we hit the peak. Pessimists predict by 2010. Optimists say not for 30 to 40 years." Jordan and Powell believe that when oil production does begin to decline, the United States and other nations that rely on oil will suffer. "Because production cannot meet demand," they maintain, "the price of oil will rapidly and continuously escalate, degrading economies and living standards. After Hubbert's Peak, $7 per gallon will seem cheap."

However, there are many critics of Hubbert's theory, who believe that current estimates of oil reserves are incorrect. They predict that as humanity creates new technology, it will continue to find new sources of oil and new methods of extracting it. As natural resources consultant Jefferson G. Edgens points out, there have long been fears over the depletion of oil, and these have usually proven to be exaggerated. For example, says Edgens, "In the 1970s, doomsayers claimed the nation would run out of energy within the next two decades." Instead, according to Edgens, "Economic growth proved these naysayers wrong. New technologies and discoveries expanded the resource pie, bringing more energy to consumers at an affordable price." According to professor David Deming, "We have not run out of oil because new technologies increase the amount of recoverable oil, and market prices—which signal scarcity—encourage new exploration and development. Rather than ending, the Oil Age has barely begun."

The extent of world oil supplies is not the only potential problem that America faces as a result of its reliance on oil for transportation. It also faces international competition for that oil. The United States is heavily dependent on foreign oil to meet its transportation needs. According to the U.S. Energy Information Administration (EIA), the country imports approximately 12 million barrels of oil every day, with approximately two-thirds of that used for transportation. Every year, that number increases, but so does the demand from other nations such as China and India. For example, according to policy experts Jerry Taylor and Peter Van Doren, between 2002 and 2004 U.S. oil consumption grew by 700,000 barrels per day, but China's consumption grew more than twice as fast as that—by 1.47 million barrels per day. It is widely believed that world oil production will not be able to keep pace with such rapidly escalating demand. Michael Klare, author of *Blood and Oil: The Dangers and Consequences of America's Petroleum Dependency*, predicts that "total world petroleum output will have to grow by about 44 million barrels per day between now and 2025—an increase of 57%—to meet anticipated demand." In his opinion, "It is hard to imagine where it will all come from."

According to Klare and others, when oil demand begins to exceed supply, the result will be fierce international competition. He believes oil conflicts will be increasingly common in the future because the United States and other nations rely so heavily on oil. Author Paul Roberts agrees. "It seems more and more likely that the race for a piece of the last big reserves of oil and natural gas will be the dominant geopolitical theme of the 21st century," he says. Roberts believes that "we are on the cusp of a new kind of war—between those who have enough energy and those who do not but are increasingly willing to go out and get it."

America's dependence on imported oil is further complicated by the fact that many of the regions containing this oil, such as the Middle East, Azerbaijan, Nigeria, and Venezuela, are torn by ethnic or religious conflict or have populations that are anti-American. According to the EIA, the United States gets approximately 25 percent of its oil from Arab members of the Organization of Petroleum Exporting Countries, 11 percent from Nigeria, and 13 percent from Venezuela. Thus, America is extremely vulnerable to any disruptions in oil supply that may result from conflicts in these often-unstable nations. In Klare's opinion, "We remain trapped in our dependence on imported oil." He warns that it is only a matter of time until this dependence has disastrous effects for the United

States. "The U.S. energy crisis may be provoked by a coup d'état in Nigeria, a civil war in Venezuela, or a feud among senior princes in the Saudi royal family," says Klare. "Or it could happen after a major act of terrorism or catastrophe climate event."

Given the rise in oil insecurity, America's dependence on the automobile is being questioned. Already, many automakers are producing gas-electric hybrids and are developing cars that run on hydrogen. Other Americans are calling for increased financing for public transportation while others are pushing for people to move closer to urban centers to reduce driving. In *Opposing Viewpoints: Cars in America*, the authors explore the changes that oil insecurity will likely affect as well as other topics related to automobiles in the following chapters: How Do Cars Affect Life in the United States? How Can Driving in America Be Made Safer? How Should Youth Driving Be Regulated? How Can the United States Meet Its Future Transportation Needs? Because of the important role cars have played in America, the growing insecurity over how to fuel them will likely have a profound effect on life in the United States.

OPPOSING
VIEWPOINTS®
SERIES

CHAPTER 1

How Do Cars Affect Life in the United States?

Chapter Preface

The automobile plays a central role in American life, perhaps more than in any other nation in the world. Indeed, the United States has more cars than any other country. According to the Earth Policy Institute, America's motor vehicle fleet, at approximately 226 million, numbers almost one car for every person. Not surprisingly, this increasing dependency on cars is having a major impact on American society. A group of people especially impacted are pedestrians, who comprise a high number of vehicle-related fatalities, and who often find it less pleasant to walk in their communities as the number of cars increases.

According to government statistics, pedestrian deaths comprise a major percentage of annual highway deaths. Approximately five thousand pedestrians die every year from being struck by automobiles—about 12 percent of total highway deaths. As *Washington Post* writer Greg Schneider explains, cars are deadly when they hit a human body. "A pedestrian steps into traffic and is hit, and the outcome is always one-sided," he states. Schneider cites Virginia police sergeant Pat Wimberly, who agrees that "whoever designed and implemented the human body never intended [it to be hit by a car.]" Sport utility vehicles (SUVs), which comprise a large percentage of vehicles sold in the United States, are even more lethal than cars to pedestrians. In 2005 researchers at Trinity College in Dublin found that the chance of killing or injuring a pedestrian is two to four times higher for someone driving an SUV than it is for the driver of a car.

In addition to causing a high number of pedestrian fatalities, an increasing number of cars means that Americans are less likely to walk in the first place. Many communities are tailored to drivers, not pedestrians, so that walking becomes more unpleasant due to pollution and noise. "Motoring freedom . . . is purchased at the cost of curtailing the freedom of pedestrians," notes the Public Transportation Users Association. It adds, "Almost everyone is affected by the pervasive pollution and noise which is a necessary condition of the freedom we enjoy as motorists." In 2003 researchers Barbara A. McCann and Reid Ewing studied a number of U.S. communities and found that Americans walk far less than they used to. For example, the authors found that "while 71 percent of parents of school-aged children walked or biked to school when they were young, only 18 percent of their children do so." Why? The authors offer an explanation: "[In] sprawling counties . . . homes are far from any other destination, and often the only route between the two may be on a busy high-speed arterial road that is unpleasant or even unsafe for . . . walking."

While it is undeniable that the automobile has had negative effects on life in the United States, many commentators note that it has also been a positive influence in many ways. To be sure, there is widespread debate on what the overall impact of the car has been. The authors in the following chapter offer various opinions on this controversial topic.

> "The car . . . is something incredibly spe-
> cial . . . that can truly be said to have
> liberated mankind."

Car Culture Gives Americans Freedom

Sam Kazman

*In the following viewpoint Sam Kazman argues that the auto-
mobile has given most Americans a freedom that they never had
before its invention. Cars allow people to move freely around the
country, says Kazman, increasing their knowledge of their world.
He points out that cars also allow greater choice in where people
live and work, and with whom they associate. Kazman is general
counsel for the Competitive Enterprise Institute, a free-market
advocacy organization in Washington, D.C. His writing has appeared in numerous publications, including the* Washington
Post, *the* Wall Street Journal, USA Today, *and* Regulation.

As you read, consider the following questions:

1. Why was the car democratized in America, in
   Kazman's opinion?
2. Why is congestion a sign of success, as explained by
   the author?
3. According to Kazman, how does the car expand economic opportunities?

Sam Kazman, "Automobility and Freedom," *Navigator*, vol. 4, September 2001. Copyright © 2001 by the Objectivist Center. All rights reserved. Reproduced by permission
of the *Navigator*, a publication of the Objectivist Center and author.

A century and a half ago, the legal scholar Sir Henry Maine observed that the evolution of human society was a movement from a society of status towards a society of contract. In traditional society, what you were depended on the circumstances of your birth. Born a serf, you remained a serf all your life. Born an aristocrat, you remained an aristocrat all your life. Modern society, however, is a society of contract, in which what you can become depends upon what you can do. In a similar way, I think, much of our recent history has involved not just evolutionary movement, but also literal movement. We've become a society of far greater physical movement. Traditionally, for most people, where you lived depended upon where you were born. Aristocrats, of course, have always been able to get around, but that was a freedom common people did not previously enjoy. What is new in this century, as a result of the automobile, is that physical mobility has become accessible to just about everyone who is free.

My essential theme is that the car is just not another consumer item, and not just a very important consumer item; rather, that it is something incredibly special, something that ranks with only a handful of other technologies that can truly be said to have liberated mankind. . . .

Cars Versus Horses

Let me begin by offering some background. The car was invented in Europe, but it was democratized in America. When Henry Ford introduced the Model T in 1909, it sold for $825. By 1925, it sold for only $260. Europe was using a carriage-trade approach toward manufacturing cars, the same as it did with horse-drawn carriages: a small group of men did everything. Consequently, in Europe, it took about 3,000 man-days to build one car. Once Henry Ford got going, it took 70 man-days. In Europe, therefore, the car was a plaything of aristocrats. America made it something everyone could afford.

Second, remember what the car replaced—horses. You think cars are dirty in terms of what they emit? A horse produces about forty-five pounds of manure per day. That's not all; in the late 1800s, New York City was disposing of 15,000 horse carcasses a year. Now, it is one thing to find a rusted hulk of a car on the roadside, but if you come upon a horse carcass, it is a different order of disgust. Then, too, if early cars were unsafe, the things they replaced were even more unsafe. Horses were not a very safe mode of transportation, and controlling them was especially a problem for women and the elderly.

Which brings me to a little side issue; the late political scientist Aaron Wildavsky observed that the world is made safer by dangerous products. These products are dangerous, they have risks, but they replace products that are *even more dangerous*. For all of the car's problems, what it replaced was a very dangerous, very dirty type of transportation, which made cities, and especially the high-density cores of cities, incredibly filthy places. . . .

The Attacks on the Car

In one sense, today's attacks are not new. When railroads were first being developed in the 1800s, the Duke of Wellington declared that they would just encourage common people to move about needlessly. Aristocrats had always been able to move about, but once commoners began to do it by rail, mobility became an object of aristocratic disdain. And once the car was developed, the disdain was not much different. In the early 1900s, one member of the British Parliament claimed that the car was a luxury that would degenerate into a nuisance. More recently, we have a whole slew of attacks on the car. [Former U.S. vice president] Al Gore, in *Earth in the Balance*, wrote that the internal combustion engine is a mortal threat to society, deadlier than any military enemy.

That message has become something we hear daily. Let me go through some television ads to illustrate.

In this first ad, a young man driving down a deserted desert road is stopped by a highway trooper who asks, rather forcefully, why he isn't car pooling. When we've shown this ad some people have thought it was a satire that we produced at the Competitive Enterprise Institute (CEI). It isn't; it is a serious environmentalist ad. The fact that, at the end, the officer does not return that kid's nervous smile indicates that it's no spoof.

In a second commercial, a troubled woman is searching for something in her home. She gets increasingly desperate as she looks, yanking open drawers and sweeping countertop items to the floor. Is she looking for cigarettes? A fix? She seems about to fall apart when she suddenly finds it—her car keys! "Addiction" is the accusation that opponents of the car often use. They don't say "our love affair with the car" or even "our over-dependence on the car." It's claimed to be an addiction. . . .

This third commercial is from Greenpeace. It shows all these toy cars assembled into the shape of a dinosaur, which then collapses while the narrator intones: "It's coming—the end of the age of the automobile." The ad closes with a pleasant scene of people biking down a city street. Notice that whenever you see the bicycle portrayed as an alternative to the car, the bike-riders are always healthy people, unburdened with shopping carts or groceries or babies. They're never elderly or handicapped. And it's never a rainy day.

"Moving About Needlessly"

Some of these ads raise issues that are conceivably valid, such as pollution and its violation of property rights. But many of the attacks on cars have nothing to do with pollution. Think back to the late 1980s, when there were news reports of a phenomenon known as cold fusion. It was supposedly a new chemical reaction that would produce limitless, totally clean, incredibly cheap energy from mechanisms operating at room temperature. For several weeks it seemed that we might really have a new form of energy. So, what did the prospect of non-polluting energy mean to the environmentalists? Let me quote Paul Ehrlich, a Stanford professor and one on the leaders of the ecology movement: "It would be like giving a machine gun to an idiot child." Jeremy Rifkin, another anti-technologist, said: "It's the worst thing that could happen to our planet." Why? Because until then, pollution was a stick with which these people could attack energy use. Once that stick was taken away, once energy became immune to these pollution-based attacks, anti-techologists would be left totally unarmed. That was the worse thing they could imagine.

Let me give you another quotation, this one from Amory Lovins, who runs the Rocky Mountain Institute and is one of the leaders of alternative "soft energy": "Suppose we had clean, renewable, hydrogen-powered, ultra-safe, 150-mile-per gallon station wagons, which we probably could have if we wanted them. What would that mean if two billion Chinese or ten million Los Angelenos drove those cars? Well, it simply wouldn't work. We might not run out of food or air, but we'd run out of roads and patience." Those quotations demonstrate that most of the philosophical antagonism towards the car has little to do with arguable claims regarding pollution and property rights. Instead, it's remarkably similar to the disdain that the Duke of Wellington expressed over a century and a half ago: the common people are moving about needlessly, if not via rail then via sport utility vehicle.

Planning Versus Choice

Nothing ruins a central-planner's vision more than a technology that lets individuals go where they want, when they want. Nothing destroys their plans the way a car does.

The Importance of Mobility

Mobility is crucial to both affluence and prosperity. A person with a car can get to a job anywhere in a sprawling modern urban area, whether Portland, Phoenix, Perth, or Paris. A person dependent on [public] transit can at best get to downtown or to within a fairly constrained area of the urban core. As for suburb-to-suburb commuting by transit, that takes time—much time—and is often not even possible.

Wendell Cox, Heartland Institute,
July 6, 2004. www.heartland.org.

Planners often begin their attacks on cars by pointing to congestion. But in the private economy, congestion is an opportunity. If you are running a restaurant and you get a good review in the local newspaper, then all of a sudden crowds are lined up outside at dinnertime. That's an opportunity for you, and you'll respond to it by accommodating the increased demand. You'll introduce early-bird specials to get some people to come at off-peak times. You may even expand your restaurant, or build another. Congestion is a visible symbol that your place is a success. Yet planners insist that highway congestion is a sign of failure. It is not. It becomes a sign of failure and causes problems for highways only because those highways are political infrastructures, not privately managed institutions.

What do critics of the car think that we ought to do about congestion? What is the vision they offer? They want us to prevent congestion and sprawl by going back to the European-style high-density city life. But this is an issue of lifestyle, not property rights. The fact is that people, for decades, for many reasons, have been moving away from cities. Sometimes they decide to move back. Regardless, they are engaging in choices of lifestyle, not in violations of rights. But to the central planner, and to those who believe in centrally planned societies, nothing could be more disturbing.

The National Association of Home Builders polled people on this question: If you were given the choice between an urban townhouse, close to public transportation, close to shopping and work versus a single-family, detached home in an outlying suburb, which would you chose? Eighty-three percent went for the single family home; seventeen percent for the urban townhouse. Many people do not like the urban style of living, or at least they do not want it for certain phases of their life such as when they are going to raise kids. . . .

A Philosophical Examination of Automobility

The car's connection to freedom of physical motion may seem obvious, but Professor [Loren] Lomasky [of Bowling Green State University in Ohio] examines its less obvious contribution to several other aspects as well.

One of these involves knowledge. Philosophers sometimes distinguish between knowledge by description and knowledge by acquaintance. Knowledge by description is what you learn from reading, knowledge by acquaintance is what you learn from experience. You can do all the reading you want about Chicago, you can read everything you want about it, and maybe view everything on the Web. But if you tell someone, "I really know Chicago," and they ask, "Have you ever been there?" and you say no, it is clear that you've been pulling their leg. Much knowledge, especially of actual locales, is acquired by going and seeing. For intermediate ranges, even for some very long distances, nothing exceeds the ability of a car to allow a person to do that. When it comes to your city, the outlying areas, the farms within a day's trip, nothing enables you to know them like the car. There may be exceptions, such as the densely populated core areas of certain cities where you might learn far more by walking, but for most of the world, at least the paved world, the best way is going to be the car.

Another liberating aspect of the car involves the issue of privacy. When you get into your car and close the door, you have incredible control over your environment, such as what you listen to and whom, if anyone, you're with. It may well exceed the bathroom as a privacy-enhancing chamber of twentieth-century life.

But the car also allows people to achieve privacy in another way. The dense, urban lifestyle is something that a lot of people do not like, and quite often that includes immigrants to this country who have left precisely that style of life. . . .

Lastly, the automobile vastly expands your range of economic opportunities. Throughout most of history, where you lived was pretty much where you worked. That changed somewhat with the Industrial Revolution; the question then became: Where could you move to in order to work and live? But only with the car was there a true disaggregation of the two. With the car, working in one place still left you free to live in a huge range of other places. And if you lost a job in one place, you no longer had to pull up roots and move. Being able to choose where we live is incredibly important, because in large part we are choosing who most of our friends are going to be. . . .

The Path to Freedom

Let me conclude with this thought. We have all heard the phrase about people voting with their feet. Automobile use is a matter of people voting with their tires. Mobility is an incredibly important ability. When [economist] Friedrich Hayek wrote *The Road to Serfdom*,[1] it seemed like that was the road that civilization was truly taking. But it is clear now that we are on a different road, a road from serfdom. For many people that road starts as a footpath; it starts as one that they take on

1. 1944 book critiquing socialism and favoring free-market capitalism

their bloodied feet. For lots of us, though, that road eventually turns into an actual highway. That's what is in the balance in this debate. As convenient as driving may be, it is much, much more than that. It is a lovely activity, and a moral activity, and control over it is one of the last things you would want to give up to any government.

> "Car culture . . . no longer represents ei-
> ther privilege or progress."

Car Culture Does Not Give Americans Freedom

Jay Walljasper

Many people see cars as a symbol of freedom and mobility, but in fact automobiles reduce mobility and restrict freedom, says Jay Walljasper in the following viewpoint. Automobiles foster dependence, he claims, forcing people to drive through increasingly crowded streets and highways. Walljasper argues that cars also create pollution and congestion, which actually reduces people's quality of life.

Walljasper is editor at large for Utne *magazine. He also writes a series for the* Nation *magazine about positive social and political initiatives, and a column on political and environmental topics for* Resurgence, Shambhala Sun, *and* Conscious Choice *magazines.*

As you read, consider the following questions:

1. According to Walter Hook, as quoted by the author, how do pedestrians suffer when automobiles come to dominate a nation's streets?

2. According to Walljasper, why does Prague have one of the highest car ownership rates in the world?

3. In the author's opinion, how has car culture recently changed in London, Madrid, and Rome?

I am sitting in the back of a motionless taxi on the way from New York's JFK [John F. Kennedy] airport to a meeting in the city. It's a blazing hot spring morning—a preview of global warming, I wonder? I felt vaguely guilty about hailing a cab to research a story on innovative ideas in transportation, especially when I knew that a new train connection from the airport had recently opened, but I didn't want to be late for my appointment. Yet now here I am stuck in traffic, and it isn't even rush hour.

My taxi driver, recently arrived from India, knows a few tricks. He edges the cab toward an exit ramp and then barrels along city streets for a few blocks before heading back onto a slightly less congested stretch of the expressway. His radio is tuned to traffic reports—a long litany of pile-ups, closed lanes, construction delays, or inexplicable slowdowns on most major roads. "It's one big parking lot out there," the announcer says, and I suddenly feel an exhaust-induced burning at the back of my throat.

"How's that new Air Train to the airport?" I casually ask the driver just after he'd swerved off the expressway again and nearly sideswiped a hapless pedestrian who dared to cross the street. "People don't want to take trains," he declares in a voice that clearly indicates this portion of our conversation is over. We fight endless tides of traffic all the way to Manhattan. Sixty minutes and forty-five dollars later, I arrive at the offices of the Institute for Transportation and Development Policy (ITDP) thirty-eight minutes late.

Fascination with Automotive Mobility

I sometimes find it hard to believe there could be any more cars in the world than there are today. Yet if economic forecasts are to be believed, auto use will rise dramatically in coming years as emerging middle-class households in China,

India, and even Africa achieve the universal dream of owning their own means of transportation.

People everywhere are enraptured by the idea of personal mobility that automobiles seem to offer—a love affair best evoked in an anecdote told by Song Laoshi, a teacher in Beijing, to a British journalist: "When I was a child, we used to walk miles to the nearest road and then just stand and wait. You will never guess why. We wanted a car to pass so that we could breathe in the fumes. For us, that was really exciting."

"Of course everybody is fascinated by cars," says Walter Hook, executive director of ITDP, which promotes sustainable transportation projects throughout the developing world. "I am too. I just love those Cooper Minis. They're beautiful."

Alternatives to Cars

"But I don't buy this business that car culture is unstoppable," he adds. "Sure, people in the developing world dream of owning cars, but they also want beautiful public places, a metro, bike lanes, pedestrian zones and sidewalk cafes. What they want is to be Paris, not look like some American suburb."

Hook knows quite a lot about both suburban America— where he grew up outside Washington, D.C., and at age 16 abandoned his bicycle for a speedy car—and the developing world, where he fell back in love with biking when working for an import-export firm in China. He now cycles through New York's heavy traffic most days, except when he's in Asia, Africa or Latin America advocating the idea of balanced transportation policies—which means that governments invest in transit, sidewalks and bikeways, rather than pouring all their money into more roads.

Working with branch offices in Ghana and Senegal, an affiliate group in Berlin, and field staff in India, Indonesia, South Africa, Brazil and Colombia, ITDP undertakes practical projects like equipping African health workers and tsunami relief volunteers with bicycles, promoting the rickshaw as a sustainable alternative to cars in Asian cities, and advising municipal officials everywhere on building 21st Century bus systems.

Hook emphasizes that sustainable transportation is not only an environmental concern, but a question of justice. "We need to remember that owning a car is out of reach for all but the upper 20 percent of people in the developing world," he notes. And when automobiles come to dominate a nation's streets, non-motorists—even if they comprise a large majority of the population—suffer in terms of both mobility and safety. Walking and biking become too dangerous. Hook notes more than 50 percent of road fatalities in some developing nations are pedestrians.

A Symbol of Privilege and Progress

"You can't just force people not to drive," Steven Logan, editor of *Car Busters* magazine, tells me as we sprint across a street in Prague where motorists actually seem to speed up when seeing us in the crosswalk. We are walking to the office of the World Carfree Network—a collective of young Europeans and North Americans who publish *Car Busters* magazine and enthusiastically promote visions of a world with fewer automobiles.

"If someone in India wants a car, sure, I can tell them it's better to take a train," he adds, "But they can say, 'Yeah, you grew up with cars and now you don't want me to have one.'"

Logan, 30, concedes he had his own car as a teenager in suburban Toronto and drove it to high school every day even though the school was only a short bike ride from home. But spending a semester abroad in Amsterdam, he discovered he could live a modern, fulfilling life without a car. "It was great. I biked everywhere," he recalls. "Then I went home to the suburbs of Toronto, and found I was really depressed."

In Servitude to the Car

Never have Americans suffered more from the kingdom of the car, nor been more in servitude to it. Buying approximately 1 million motor vehicles a month, we have doubled traffic on the nation's roads in the last two decades. Today, the two or three cars owned by half of all American families gridlock our lives and landscape.

The impact of congestion, however, has gone far beyond the commute that made rush hour the opposite of its name. We use a scant 22 percent of our vehicle-miles to take us to the office. Vacation travel, the other reason we give for owning this pricey vehicle, devours a scant eight percent of our journeys.

In fact, two-thirds of the miles we drive go to chauffeuring and consuming by car. Car bonding? Hardly.

Jane Holtz Kay, Culture Change,
n.d. www.culturechange.org.

After several more harrowing encounters with Prague's burgeoning car culture, we arrive at the World Carfree Network office—a cramped apartment in a modest neighborhood far from the picturesque center of the city that serves as the newsroom for *Car Busters* and world headquarters for a coalition of more than 50 sustainable-transportation groups in 27 countries on six continents. "Our overall principle is that the automobile should not determine how we build our communities," says Network co-founder Randy Ghent, 32, a refugee from the auto-dominated suburbs of California. He detects signs of a post-car culture emerging from what's happening in Bogotá, in the new virtually car-free neighborhoods created in Amsterdam, Hamburg, Edinburgh, and Vienna as well as a car-free community being discussed for the San Francisco Bay area, not far from his hometown. The Internet, he muses, might easily replace the automobile as humanity's dream of unlimited mobility.

"We don't have to go back to the past and re-create the medieval city," Ghent explains. "If we can get more examples of car-free places, maybe by converting an old military base into a new town, then people can see a car-free community side by side with an auto-dependent neighborhood. That could lead to big change."

But what about Prague? I ask. It's got a world-class subway, trams going all over town and a breathtakingly beautiful car-free city center which draws visitors from all over the world. Yet it also sports one of the highest car-ownership rates in Europe. Lutra Lebrova, 27, World Carfree Nework's co-director, who grew up in the Czech Republic, steps in to explain. "It was really hard to get a car under Communism. People had to wait 10 or 12 years, and everyone now is so proud of their cars. People here see it as their special right to drive cars."

This helps me understand the scary habits of Prague drivers, and also sheds light on a broader truth about the powerful appeal of automobiles. In most cultures around the world cars offer a potent symbol of privilege and progress. Motorists in these places think of themselves as the future, and anyone who gets in the way of the future had better watch out.

The Desire for Mobility

The truth is that humans have an innate urge to increase their personal mobility, which cannot be deterred no matter how alarming the statistics about traffic fatalities or global warming seem. A world offering more car-free places, will only happen when people come to realize automobiles actually stand in the way of greater mobility and a better life.

It's helpful to remember that before there was Prague, with its fiercely reckless drivers, or Bangkok and Jakarta, with their horrendous traffic jams, the picture of a transportation nightmare in most people's minds was Rome, Madrid or London. In each of these places, autos represented something deeper than just a way to get around. In Rome of the '60s, car culture was a mark of Italy's arrival as a prosperous nation; in Madrid of the '70s, a badge of the modern consumer society that replaced Franco's dictatorship; and in London of the '80s, the supreme symbol of free-market freedom as defined by [former British prime minister] Margaret Thatcher.

But look at them now. London shocked the world with the huge success of its congestion pricing policy, which charges drivers a hefty fee to enter the city centre. Madrid has tamed its famously unruly traffic with aggressive implementation of pedestrian streets and other measures to keep cars from ruining neighborhoods. And Rome, the butt of so many jokes about impossible traffic and insane drivers, has reduced traffic by 25 percent in its centre—an initiative that has become the model for Paris, a city usually looked to as the urban ideal.

Just Another Way to Get Around

Hazarding a guess about the future is always risky, especially when the outcome of your prediction directly affects powerful interests like the auto and oil industries, but I believe the feisty sustainable transportation movement is on to something big. "People say cars represent freedom but how free are you when you have to drive everywhere?" asks Steven Logan of *Car Busters*, answering his own question. "Gas is expensive. The roads are congested. I find it very liberating to be out somewhere and know I can easily walk home."

Following in the footsteps (rather than the tire tracks) of Rome and Madrid and London, I believe people in Eastern Europe and Asia and someday even North America—where car culture was born and remains stubbornly embedded—will eventually discover an important truth: The auto is at its best and its most useful as just one of many ways to get around.

This revelation hit home for me the day I was stuck in the back seat of a New York taxi. I vowed then and there to try the new Air Train when returning to the airport. My train ride back to JFK, which cost a total of seven bucks, was smooth and simple, even at rush hour, and I arrived quite early for my flight. Car culture, I decided while relaxing over a meal and glass of wine in the airport lounge, no longer represents either privilege or progress.

"*People in sprawling areas may be missing out on significant health benefits that are available simply by . . . getting physical activity as part of everyday life.*"

Urban Sprawl Resulting from Cars Contributes to Obesity

Barbara A. McCann and Reid Ewing

In the following viewpoint Barbara A. McCann and Reid Ewing report that people who live in sprawling counties are likely to walk less than people living in more compact communities. In sprawling developments walking or bicycling is often inconvenient or dangerous, they explain, increasing the likelihood that people will drive to reach a destination. McCann and Ewing believe that this decreased physical activity causes an increased incidence of obesity and chronic diseases such as hypertension and high blood pressure. They recommend that communities be reshaped in order to encourage walking and biking instead of driving. McCann is a writer and public policy expert on the impact of the built environment on public health and quality of life. Ewing is a research professor at the National Center for Smart Growth at the University of Maryland.

As you read, consider the following questions:

1. According to the authors, how much more were people in the most sprawling areas studied likely to weigh than people in the most compact county?

2. As cited by McCann and Ewing, what percentage of Americans would like to walk more instead of driving?

3. According to the authors, how many deaths each year are caused by physical inactivity and being overweight?

Health experts agree: most Americans are too sedentary and weigh too much. Obesity has reached epidemic levels, and diseases associated with inactivity are also on the rise. What is creating this public health crisis? Much of the focus to date has been on whether Americans are eating too much fattening food. But researchers are starting to pay attention to the other half of the weight-gain equation: Americans' low levels of physical activity. A pressing question for public health officials is whether the design of our communities makes it more difficult for people to get physical activity and maintain a healthy weight.

This report presents the first national study to show a clear association between the type of place people live and their activity levels, weight, and health. The study, *Relationship Between Urban Sprawl and Physical Activity, Obesity, and Morbidity*, found that people living in counties marked by sprawling development are likely to walk less and weigh more than people who live in less sprawling counties. In addition, people in more sprawling counties are more likely to suffer from hypertension (high blood pressure). These results hold true after controlling for factors such as age, education, gender, and race and ethnicity.

Researchers measured the degree of sprawl with a county 'sprawl index' that used data available from the US Census Bureau and other federal sources to quantify development patterns in 448 counties in urban areas across the United States. Counties with a higher degree of sprawl received a lower numerical value on the index, and county sprawl index scores range from 63 for the most sprawling county to 352 for the least sprawling county. Sprawling counties are spread-out areas where homes are far from any other destination, and often the only route between the two may be on a busy high-speed arterial road that is unpleasant or even unsafe for biking or walking. People who live in these areas may find that driving is the most convenient way to get everything done, and they are less likely to have easy opportunities to walk, bicycle, or take transit as part of their daily routine.

Indeed, previous research has shown that people living in sprawling areas drive more, while people living in compact communities are more likely to walk. Medical research has shown that walking and similar moderate physical activity is important to maintaining healthy weight and bestows many other health benefits. What is groundbreaking about this study is that it is the first national study to establish a direct association between the form of the community and the health of the people who live there.

Analysis Shows Sprawl Is Linked to Health

The study compared the county sprawl index to the health characteristics of more than 200,000 individuals living in the 448 counties studied, using a large national health survey, the Behavioral Risk Factor Surveillance System (BRFSS), which is maintained by the Centers for Disease Control and Prevention (CDC).

The results show that people in more sprawling counties are likely to have a higher body mass index (BMI), a standard measure of weight-to-height that is used to determine if people are overweight or obese. A 50-point increase in the degree of sprawl on the county sprawl index was associated with a weight gain of just over one pound for the average person. Looking at the extremes, the people living in the most sprawling areas are likely to weigh six pounds more than people in the most compact county. . . . Obesity, defined as a BMI of 30 or higher, followed a similar pattern. The odds that a county resident will be obese rises ten percent with every 50-point increase in the degree of sprawl on the county sprawl index.

The study also found a direct relationship between sprawl and chronic disease. The odds of having hypertension, or high blood pressure, are six percent higher for every 50-point increase in the degree of sprawl. The 25 most sprawling counties had average hypertension rates of 25 per 100 while the 25 least sprawling had hypertension rates of 23 per 100. The researchers did not find any statistically significant association between community design and diabetes or cardiovascular disease. While all three chronic conditions are associated with being inactive and overweight, many other factors including heredity may moderate the relationship between sprawl and chronic diseases.

People in sprawling areas walk less for exercise, which may help explain the higher obesity levels. But routine daily activity, such as walking for errands, may have a bigger role. When the researchers controlled for the amount of walking for exercise that people reported, they found that people in more sprawling counties weigh more whether or not they walk for exercise. This suggests that people in sprawling areas may be missing out on significant health benefits that are available simply by walking, biking, climbing stairs, and getting physical activity as part of everyday life.

These results point toward the need to continue investigating how our communities may be affecting our health. Additional studies are needed to better understand the relationship between sprawling development and the risk of being overweight, and to more precisely measure physical activity.

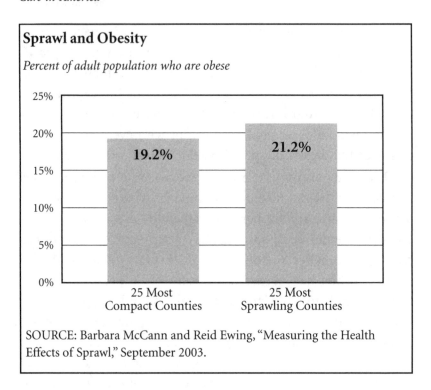

Sprawl and Obesity

Percent of adult population who are obese

SOURCE: Barbara McCann and Reid Ewing, "Measuring the Health Effects of Sprawl," September 2003.

Creating Healthy Communities

We know that people would like to have more opportunities to walk and bicycle: recent national polls found that 55 percent of Americans would like to walk more instead of driving, and 52 percent would like to bicycle more. Leaders looking to reshape their communities to make it easier to walk and bicycle have many options. They can invest in improved facilities for biking and walking, install traffic calming measures to slow down cars, or create Safe Routes to School programs that focus on helping kids walk and bike to school. They also can create more walkable communities by focusing development around transit stops, retrofitting sprawling neighborhoods, and revitalizing older neighborhoods that are already walkable. When paired with programs that educate people about the benefits of walking, these changes can help increase physical activity.

Addressing these issues is essential both for personal health and for the long-term health of our communities. Physical inactivity and being overweight are factors in over 200,000 premature deaths each year. The director of the CDC recently said obesity might soon overtake tobacco as the nation's number-one health threat. Meanwhile, rising health care costs are threatening state budgets. Getting decision makers to consider how the billions spent on transportation and development can make communities more walkable and bikeable is one avenue to improving the health and quality of life of millions of Americans.

| "Sprawl probably had very little to do with [America's increasing obesity rates]."

There Is No Link Between Urban Sprawl and Obesity

Wendell Cox and Ronald D. Utt

In the following viewpoint Wendell Cox and Ronald D. Utt charge that the conclusions of a study by Smart Growth America linking sprawl and obesity are flawed. The results of the study have been vastly exaggerated by planners opposed to sprawl, maintain Cox and Wendell. In reality, they argue, the study showed a trivial link between sprawling communities and rates of obesity. In addition, they point out, while obesity has increased in the past decade, sprawl has not, meaning that sprawl is highly unlikely to be the cause. Cox is principal of the Wendell Cox Consultancy in St. Louis, Missouri, and a visiting fellow at the Heritage Foundation. Utt is Herbert and Joyce Morgan senior research fellow at the Thomas A. Roe Institute for Economic Policy Studies at the Heritage Foundation.

As you read, consider the following questions:

1. According to the authors, what did a Rutgers University researcher admit about the findings of the Smart Growth America study?

Wendell Cox and Ronald D. Utt, "Sprawl and Obesity: A Flawed Connection," *Heritage Foundation WebMemo #337*, September 19, 2003. Copyright © 2003 by The Heritage Foundation. Reproduced by permission.

2. How many more people choose to live in less dense suburban communities than in dense places like Manhattan, as argued by Cox and Utt?

3. According to the authors, how might income and weight be related?

A new report from Smart Growth America and the Surface Transportation Policy Project [STPP], *Measuring the Health Effects of Sprawl*, links growing obesity concerns with sprawl. The report's findings, however, fall short of supporting this conclusion.

Instead, this is another attempt by the report's sponsors to spin research showing only trivial weight differences between city and suburban residents into a national crisis requiring land use restrictions.

From Boston to Canberra, the headlines told the message: "America's expanding obesity tied to sprawl." The study purports to demonstrate that people living in more sprawling, suburban counties are fatter than people who live in more dense central cities. The principal cause of this reported difference is that people walk more in cities than suburbs, where there is greater dependency on cars.

But what may be most revealing about the report is not the report's conclusions, but the apparent desperation of the sponsors who felt obligated to publicize research showing that there are only trivial weight differences between cities and suburban residents. A better headline would have been: "Researchers demonstrate statistically significant insignificance."

Manipulating Data

Using survey data from the Centers for Disease Control [CDC] from 445 counties around the country, the researchers then applied a county sprawl index to the data and developed a computer program to predict the weight and obesity of people in the counties by degree of sprawl, and then compare the prediction to the actual. After so manipulating the data, their findings proved to be "statistically significant," a mathematically determined condition meaning that the formula they developed appears to have a high probability of being reliable for predicting purposes.

But statistical significance is not enough: the results must also be material, which in this case they are not. The researchers predict, for example, that the average Cook County (Chicago) resident weighs 0.9 pounds (15 ounces) less than suburbanites in Lake County, Illinois. In effect, sprawl in Chicago can be said to add less than a pound to a suburbanite's weight. The researchers discover similarly trivial findings across the country. For the country as a whole and comparing citizen weight in the 25 counties at either extreme of sprawl and compactness, 19.2 percent of residents in the least sprawling communities were obese, while 21.2 percent in the most sprawling were obese. Even the Rutgers University researcher had to admit—with or without pun intended—that "Those aren't huge differences."

But the panic driven headlines, wide coverage, and superficial stories beneath them indicated that few reporters bothered to look beyond the sponsors' press releases. Washington Post Writers Group columnist Neal Peirce characterized the report as research "scientifically linking the United States' pattern of highway-driven, sprawling, road-dependent development with the alarming epidemic of rising weight and obesity that the country's been experiencing."

Anti-Sprawl Lobby

But as public relations experts have learned, impressions are often more important than reality. So to market findings of a connection between sprawl and obesity, however insignificant, establishes a public policy connection that is anything but insignificant. Indeed, the project sponsors can even get away with characterizing their finding of "small impact," with the

A Flawed Link

Don't blame urban sprawl for America's sprawling waist-line.

That's the message from two Oregon State University researchers, who say the nation's "obesity epidemic" probably has little to do with whether people can walk from their house to a store. They've published two studies suggesting that the connection between weight and sprawl is more of a two-way street than some planners may think. . . .

[According to the researchers,] people who are overweight and sedentary tend to gravitate toward neighborhoods with fewer opportunities for walking because that's not something they value; it's not the neighborhood that makes them overweight.

Conversely, people who tend to be more fit or enjoy walking tend to choose neighborhoods that allow them to walk to stores, theaters or jobs.

Greg Bolt, Register-Guard, *September 12, 2005.*

confidence that reporters and columnists will never read far enough to see the qualifying statements. This "big headline, little story" model is an effective strategy for an anti-sprawl lobby that would force us out of our cars and make us live on top of one another.

And that's precisely the point. Most Americans live in urban population densities of 4,000 per square mile or less. The "walkable communities" that the anti-sprawl lobby want us to create and live in exist principally in the four densest boroughs of New York City (Manhattan, the Bronx, Brooklyn and Queens). Here, population densities are from 20,000 to 70,000 per square mile. This is where the Smart Growth America-STPP researchers predict the lowest obesity rates.

Even there, however, the predicted weight difference between Manhattan (70,000 per square mile) and Queens (20,000 per square mile) is more than the difference between Queens and the most sprawling suburban county in the New York metropolitan area. Indeed, according to New York City's Department of Health and Mental Hygiene, 24 percent of the adults living in the walkable Bronx were obese compared to 21 percent nationwide, which is also precisely the proportion of obese people found in walkable Brooklyn.

The report, however, goes on to suggest that planners should design urban areas for walkability to address the problem of rising obesity. But what they don't say is that Manhattan style walkability cannot be achieved without Manhattan densities. If urban areas were the playthings of planners who could decree a corner grocery store here, a wine shop there and a Starbucks across the street, perhaps it would be different. But it is not. In fact, Manhattan is a wonderful place to live for people who want to live there. But so are suburban communities like Simi Valley, Maple Valley, Chesterfield and Alpharetta. Approximately 1.5 million people choose to live in Manhattan, and 7.5 million in the four dense boroughs of New York City. At the same time, more than 30 times as many people choose to live in places that have far more room. Public policy should not assume the nanny-role of requiring community designs that conspire to increase walking, particularly when it leads to weight differences of such trivial magnitude.

Analytical Gaps

And, while the report's findings are trivial, the analytical gaps are big enough to drive a subway train through. Researchers did not, for example, consider the relationship between income and weight, despite some evidence that the connection between the two is more significant than the one between weight and suburbs. In New York City, for example, 22 percent of people earning less than $25,000 per year were obese, compared to 15 percent of those earning over $50,000. This omission might have been justifiable if the data were not available, but it is, in the very same dataset the researchers used. Inclusion of the income variable is likely to have made the sprawl/weight results even less consequential than they are already.

Then there is the temporal connection. How can the latest iteration of sprawl (the previous one began with the advent of electric trolleys), which began the day after World War II ended, be a principal cause of the obesity explosion, which has largely emerged in only the last 10 or 15 years? Over the past decade America has not sprawled more, indeed, there have been population increases in some of the densest urban areas. Americans are not driving much more than they did a decade ago, nor is there any evidence that they are walking less. Not many more people are avoiding transit today than 10 years ago. Yet, over the past decade or so, obesity, by CDC data, has nearly doubled. And as the researchers' findings reveal, sprawl probably had very little to do with it.

"SUVs have a dark side. They spew out 47 percent more . . . air pollution than an average car."

Sport Utility Vehicles Harm America

Sierra Club

Sport utility vehicles (SUVs) threaten the environment and human health, maintains the Sierra Club in the following viewpoint. According to the organization, these vehicles are a major contributor to the greenhouse gases that cause global warming. In addition, argues the Sierra Club, SUVs pose a threat to America's natural resources because they increase the need for oil drilling in remote areas. Finally, according to the organization, SUVs are also harmful to Americans because they increase the risk of rollovers and fatal crashes on the highway. The Sierra Club is an environmental organization that works to protect earth's ecosystems and natural resources.

As you read, consider the following questions:

1. As argued by the author, how much more likely is an SUV to roll over in an accident than a car is?
2. What percentage of the vehicle market is comprised of SUVs, minivans, and light trucks, according to the Sierra Club?

3. Why do SUVs increase the risk of oil spills, as explained by the author?

W hen it comes to wasting energy, SUVs [sport utility vehicles] are unrivaled. Built with outdated, gas-guzzling technology, many SUVs get just 13 miles per gallon. And the higher gas prices are, the more money they waste.

Auto-industry advertising portrays SUVs as the ticket to freedom and the great outdoors. Commercials depict them climbing massive snow-capped mountains or tearing through desert sand dunes, taking their owners into the wild. In reality, the only off-road action many of these vehicles see is accidentally driving through a flower bed next to the driveway.

Missing from these ads are other contributions from SUVs—the brown haze of air pollution hanging over many of our national parks, images of weather disasters linked to global warming or the oil derricks and tankers needed to feed gas-guzzling SUVs. In contrast to Detroit's carefully crafted image, SUVs have a dark side. They spew out 43 percent more global-warming pollution and 47 percent more air pollution than an average car. SUVs are four times more likely than cars to roll over in an accident and three times more likely to kill the occupants in a rollover. They also cost the owner thousands more on gasoline.

Worsening the Threat of Global Warming

Because the government classifies SUVs as "light trucks" rather than cars, SUVs have a license to guzzle more gas and pollute more than cars. In 1975, when fuel-economy standards were first adopted, "light truck" referred to a vehicle used to haul hay on the farm or gravel at a construction site. At that time, light trucks comprised only 20 percent of the vehicle market. Today, SUVs, mini-vans and other light trucks make up nearly half of new vehicles sold. They are far more likely to haul lattés home from Starbucks than lumber from the yard. Even though Detroit has technology that could make them both cleaner and safer, SUVs and other light trucks are still held to low environmental standards, roll over more than cars and pose greater danger to other vehicles than cars do.

The world's leading climate scientists have warned that there is now 30 percent more carbon dioxide—the primary global-warming gas—in the atmosphere than a century ago. The burning of fossil fuels is the primary source of this CO_2 pollution. Over the same period of time, the average surface temperature of the earth has risen more than 1 degree Fahrenheit.

Due to these changes, we are already seeing signs of global warming. The 1990s was the hottest decade on record and the 11 hottest years on record have all occurred in the past 13 years.

Extreme drought conditions and changing rainfall patterns have occurred across the country, setting the stage for wildfires, which decimated areas from Florida to California. Record heat waves have killed hundreds in Chicago and infectious-disease outbreaks linked to global warming have sickened or killed hundreds from Texas to New York, shut down Disney World and re-introduced Americans to dengue fever, malaria and encephalitis. Sea levels have risen between four and 10 inches and glacial ice is rapidly retreating on five continents.

The world's leading scientists warn that over the 21st century, CO_2 levels are expected to double, raising sea levels two feet or more, worsening smog and leaving our children to cope with a more hostile climate.

America's cars and light trucks alone produce nearly 20 percent of U.S. CO_2 pollution. That's more than all but four countries worldwide! And transportation is the fastest-growing sector of global-warming pollution in the nation. Popular light trucks pump out 237 million tons of global-warming pollution into our atmosphere each year. That's because every

'I just feel so safe in my four-wheel drive.'

Cluff. © by CartoonStock Ltd. www.CartoonStock.com. Reproduced by permission.

gallon of gas burned emits 28 pounds of CO_2 into the atmosphere.

SUVs Emit More Air Pollution than Cars

Nearly 117 million Americans live in areas where the air is unhealthy to breathe, according to the American Lung Association. Light trucks, which can spew up to three times more smog-forming pollution than cars, magnify this growing health threat. The increased air pollution can lead to more asthma, bronchitis and other health problems. . . .

The U.S. Environmental Protection Agency adopted new "Tier 2" tailpipe pollution standards in 1999 to cut smog (but not CO_2) from cars and SUVs. However, these rules will not go into effect until 2004 and the auto industry has until 2009 to clean up its largest SUVs.

SUVs Threaten Our Wilderness and Coasts

A hidden cost of SUVs is the price we pay with our natural resources. To keep these gas guzzlers running, oil companies seek to drill in new areas—including some of our nation's most sensitive wilderness habitats. As the number of gas guzzlers on the road grows, so does the pressure to drill in Alaska's Arctic National Wildlife Refuge—one of the last remaining pristine ecosystems. Fragile coastlines in California and Florida, and lands surrounding Yellowstone National Park are also targets for drilling.

The *Exxon Valdez* disaster serves as a powerful reminder that transporting oil also threatens our environment.[1] Smaller spills and leaks occur daily, putting waterways and wildlife at risk. . . .

Fuel Efficiency Standards

Congress passed the Corporate Average Fuel Economy (CAFE) standards in 1975 to reduce our dangerous oil dependence. This doubled the fuel economy of America's vehicle fleet, saving 3 million barrels of oil per day. However, the oil savings from CAFE standards are being eroded by people driving farther and the rising proportion of inefficient SUVs and other light trucks. In fact, the average fuel economy of new vehicles has sunk to the lowest level since 1980. Raising the CAFE standard for light trucks to equal that of cars (27.5 mpg) would save 1 million barrels of oil per day. We can do even better. Raising the average for cars to 45 mpg and light trucks to 34 mpg would save 3 million barrels of oil per day. . . .

Rollovers and Dangers to Others on the Road

Here's what the *New York Times* said about SUV safety (July 15, 1999): "Because it is taller, heavier and more rigid, an SUV or a pickup is more than twice as likely as a car to kill the driver of the other vehicle in a collision. Yet partly because these so-called light trucks roll over so often, their occupants

---

1. In 1989 this oil tanker spilled millions of gallons of oil in Prince William Sound in the Gulf of Alaska, resulting in massive environmental damage.

have roughly the same chance as car occupants of dying in a crash."

SUVs give a false impression of safety. With their height and comparatively narrow tire-track width, SUVs handle and maneuver much less effectively than cars. Emergency swerves to avoid a crash can themselves lead to rollover accidents in SUVs, which are four times more likely to roll over in an accident. Rollovers account for 62 percent of SUV deaths but only 22 percent in cars. Yet automakers continue to fight new standards that would protect occupants in rollover accidents.

Because SUVs are built on high, stiff frames, their bumpers ride above the occupant-protecting frame of cars. When an SUV and a car collide, this height difference, combined with the stiff battering-ram frame and greater mass, create a lethal weapon.

According to a government study, in 1996 "at least 2,000 car occupants would not have been killed, had their cars collided with other cars instead of trucks of the same weight." And SUVs are also more deadly to pedestrians, bicyclists and motorcyclists than cars, in part because existing braking standards for SUVs are weaker than for cars. . . .

The Biggest Single Step

It is time for action. Please urge your public officials to support cleaning up our cars and light trucks. . . . Tell them our children have a right to a safe and healthy environment. It's time to take the biggest single step to curb global warming.

"Big government has inadvertently made SUVs and minivans the only vehicles that can accommodate many families."

Sport Utility Vehicles Do Not Harm America

Matthew Craig

Matthew Craig responds in the following viewpoint to charges that drivers of sport utility vehicles (SUVs) contribute to environmental degradation. He contends that increasing the fuel efficiency of these popular vehicles could actually increase pollution; because the vehicles would be cheaper to run, Americans would be encouraged to drive more, thus increasing auto emissions. Craig also counters the claim that SUVs are involved in more rollovers and crashes than other cars, contending that they are actually safer to drive because they are heavier. Finally, he maintains that due to government safety regulations, such as requiring that children under five years of age be restrained in child seats, SUVs are the only vehicles that can accommodate many American families. Craig is a research associate with the National Center for Public Policy Research, an organization that believes in free-market solutions to public policy problems.

As you read, consider the following questions:

    1. According to Craig, what recommendation does the

Matthew Craig, "Anti-SUV Activists Versus the American Family," *National Policy Analysis*, vol. 481, August 2003. Copyright © 2003 by the National Center for Public Policy Research. Reproduced by permission.

federal government make concerning child passengers under twelve years of age?

2. What is the occupant fatality rate for front, side, and rear crashes in SUVs compared to passenger cars, as cited by the author?

3. As related by the author, how have radical environmental groups responded to the popularity of SUVs?

When you get behind the wheel of your SUV [sport utility vehicle] or minivan, do you automatically become a member of a hate group? According to the radicals now dominating the environmental movement, driving one of these vehicles proves you hate the planet.

To the contrary: SUV and minivan owners are often law-abiding American families that are simply obeying the law.

A Necessity for Families

While the owners of compact and hybrid cars can smugly believe they are saving the world and saving money at the gas pump, their choice of vehicle is not for everyone. SUV-haters fail to understand the needs of the average American family and these vehicles are now more popular than traditional passenger cars.

In many ways, government programs make SUVs and minivans necessary.

Regulations in many states require children five years and younger (seven years and younger in New Jersey, Pennsylvania and Washington, D.C.) to be restrained in child seats at all times. Furthermore, the federal government recommends that children under 12 ride in the backseat. This literally makes it impossible for a family with four kids to fit into a traditional passenger car, let alone bring along any of their young friends.

Critics characterize SUV and minivan owners as wannabe survivalists wasting gas and clogging the roads with unsafe vehicles. However, when driven properly, SUVs and minivans are actually safer than cars. For front, side and rear crashes,

Pollution Machines

Environmentalists argue that dirtier SUVs are creating an intense new air-pollution burden on cities, and contributing to global warming because they emit more carbon dioxide than do more fuel-efficient vehicles. As one environmentalist group puts it: "Sport utility vehicles can spew 30% more carbon monoxide and hydrocarbons and 75% more nitrogen oxides than passenger cars." . . .

Yet, even as SUVs have come to dominate new car sales, air quality has improved. According to the Environmental Protection Agency, the amount of nitrogen oxide in the air dropped 11% between 1992 and 2001. Ozone dropped 3%. Carbon monoxide was down 38%. Those gains came not only as the car market shifted over towards more SUVs, minivans, and light trucks, but as cars overall were driven more. Miles traveled over the past 10 years climbed 30%. The reason may be similar to the reason for the improvements seen over the past decade in overall fuel economy. A driver who trades in a dirty old car for a slightly less polluting new SUV has helped improve the environment, even if the SUV isn't the cleanest new car coming off the assembly line.

John Merline, Consumers' Research Magazine, *April 2003.*

fatality rate per 100,000 registered vehicles is 5.83 percent lower than for passenger cars. Simply wearing seat belts would save an additional 1,000 lives per year, while driving with common sense greatly reduces much-publicized rollover deaths.

Fuel Efficiency

These critics also want to increase the Corporate Average Fuel Economy (CAFE) standards that force manufacturers to improve gas mileage. Doing so, however, would lead to higher prices and compromise size and safety. Existing CAFE standards already are cited by the government as responsible for 2,000 traffic deaths per year. And, with every 100 pounds that CAFE standards cut from the weight of a vehicle, the annual death toll increases by approximately 300 lives.

Improving gas mileage, surprisingly, won't necessarily help the environment. According to Andrew Kleit of Pennsylvania State University, better gas mileage encourages more driving. Fuel-efficient cars that reduce the cost per mile make it cheaper to drive more. Since some pollutant levels are directly proportional to the number of miles driven, CAFE standards can actually increase pollution.

"Slanderous Rhetoric"

Faced with the increasing popularity of SUVs and minivans despite their best efforts to demonize them, some frantic environmentalists are resorting to slanderous rhetoric and even violence to try to stem the tide.

Keith Bradsher's contempt is particularly noteworthy. According to reviewer Gregg Easterbrook, writing in the *New Republic*, in his book *High and Mighty: SUVs—The World's Most Dangerous Vehicles and How They Got That Way*, Bradsher displays his concern about SUVs entering the used car market where they will be bought by "immigrants, the lower middle class, and the poor, who generally speed, run lights, drive drunk, and crash more often than the prosperous classes." This sort of generalization is dangerous and hateful, and perpetuates already problematic racial stereotypes.

In Virginia, Oregon and Pennsylvania, the eco-terrorists of the Earth Liberation Front are discouraging SUV purchases through vandalism, arson and the acidic disfigurement of SUVs at dealerships. These actions force owners to live in fear of becoming the next target of what the FBI considers to be one of the most active domestic terrorist groups.

Hurting American Families

Transportation is a modern necessity. Big government has inadvertently made SUVs and minivans the only vehicles that can accommodate many families. But those same people who advocate safety requirements that make these larger vehicles a must-have for larger families are simultaneously trying to legislate them out of existence with unsafe fuel-efficiency mandates.

While their logic is muddled, one thing is clear: if these activists succeed, American families will be hurt.

Periodical Bibliography

The following articles have been selected to supplement the diverse views presented in this chapter.

Robert D. Bullard	"Transportation Policies Leave Blacks on the Side of the Road," *Crisis*, January/February 2005.
John Cloud	"Why the SUV Is All the Rage," *Time*, February 24, 2003.
Peter J. Cooper	"Attack of the Four-Wheeled Giants," *USA Today Magazine*, March 2004.
Eric Hedegaard	"The SUV on the Couch," *Rolling Stone*, November 13, 2003.
Randy Kennedy	"The Day the Traffic Disappeared," *New York Times Magazine*, April 20, 2003.
Paul Kingsnorth and Michael Harvey	"Sports Utility Vehicles," *Ecologist*, June 2005.
Albert Koehl	"A Modest Proposal," *Alternatives Journal*, Spring 2003.
John Merline	"Why Consumers Have Been Choosing SUVs," *Consumers' Research Magazine*, April 2003.
Keith Naughton	"Cruising on Campus; Cars Are Becoming the Coolest College Accessory," *Newsweek*, August 22, 2005.
Alejandro Reuss	"Car Trouble," *Dollars & Sense*, March/April 2003
Alan Reynolds	"Energy Disinformation," *Washington Times*, June 27, 2004.
Marc Silver	"Miles Per Foot," *U.S. News & World Report*, September 12, 2005.

CHAPTER 2

How Can Driving in
America Be Made Safer?

Chapter Preface

According to the Cellular Telecommunications and Internet Association, as of June 2005 over 190 million people in the United States were cell phone users. Of the calls made from the phones, a significant percentage is made by people driving automobiles—estimates range between 40 and 70 percent. As that percentage continues to increase, there is fierce debate over whether or not cell phones make America's roadways more dangerous, and if so, what to do about it. Some states have already imposed restrictions or complete bans on cell phone usage while driving. For example, New York has banned it since 2001. Other states are in the process of trying to pass bills that restrict usage. While it is desirable to make driving in America safer, as the cell phone debate reveals, suggestions on how to do so frequently generate intense disagreement.

According to the National Highway Traffic Safety Administration, 20 to 30 percent of all motor vehicle crashes are caused by driver distraction. A number of studies suggest that cell phone usage is a major distraction, and thus a major cause of traffic accidents. Researchers believe that cell phones can cause a driving distraction in three ways: visually, when a driver looks at the phone to dial or receive a call; biomechanically, when one hand is holding the phone instead of steering the car; and cognitively, when the driver is paying attention to his or her conversation and not to the road. David Ropeik and George Gray of *Consumers' Research Magazine* estimate that cell phone use by drivers causes 330,000 injuries a year, 12,000 of them serious. "There is no question that using a mobile phone while driving is a distraction," they state. "Studies of driver performance, observing drivers on both simulators and in the field, have shown that mobile phone use while driving can adversely affect reaction time, swerving ability, ability to execute difficult driving tasks, and other indicators of safe driving." A government study released in June 2005 echoes this conclusion. The study tracked one hundred cars and their drivers for a year and concluded that talking on cell phones caused far more crashes than did other distractions faced by drivers.

However, even conceding that cell phones do constitute a driving hazard, many analysts argue that restricting cell phone usage unfairly violates personal freedom. Journalist Bryan Knowles points out that in other aspects of driving, the driver is accorded a certain amount of trust. "When states issue drivers licenses, an individual motorist has been deemed both responsible and capable of making decisions behind the wheel," he says. "Holding a conversation on a cell phone while driving is no more distracting or different than talking to a passenger, eating fast food or fumbling for a music tape or CD. Motorists were involved in accidents due to inattentive driving decades before the advent of cell phones. . . . Attempts to legally prohibit this infringes on the personal rights of motorists." Matthew Edgar, research associate at the Independence Institute, cautions, "Despite the dangers of cell phone usage while driving, we ought to stop and wonder what banning cell phones while driving would do to our sense of liberty." He believes that the choice about whether or not to use cell phones while driving should be a personal one, not something the government dictates.

Cell phone usage is not the only driver safety issue that has provoked public debate in the United States. While most Americans want to reduce the number of deaths and injuries on America's roads, there is less agreement about how to accomplish that goal. The following chapter offers various opinions on the question of how driving in America can be made safer.

> "States ... should be strongly encour-
> aged to increase their safety belt use
> rates—the single most effective means
> of decreasing deaths and injuries."

Seat Belt Laws Should Be Enforced

Jeffrey W. Runge

The following viewpoint is excerpted from congressional testimony given by Jeffrey W. Runge in April 2005. He argues that car crashes are a serious problem in the United States, causing thousands of deaths and costing billions of dollars each year. Runge urges the Senate to reauthorize the Safe, Accountable, Flexible, and Efficient Transportation Equity Act (SAFETEA), which would reward states that enforce seat belt laws. In his opinion, the enforcement of seat belt laws is the single most effective way to reduce highway deaths. Runge is administrator of the National Highway Traffic Safety Administration, the government administration that works to keep America's roads safe. SAFETEA was signed into law in August 2005.

As you read, consider the following questions:

1. According to Runge, for what age group of Americans are transportation-related injuries the leading cause of death?

Jeffrey W. Runge, testimony before the U.S. Senate Subcommittee on Surface Transportation and Merchant Marine, Committee on Commerce, Science, and Transportation, Washington, DC, April 5, 2005.

2. As explained by the author, what is the average yearly cost per person for car crashes in the United States?

3. In Runge's opinion, if seat belt use increased from 80 to 90 percent, how many lives would be saved every year?

T he National Highway Traffic Safety Administration's (NHTSA) mission is to save lives and prevent injuries. Motor vehicle crashes are responsible for 95 percent of all transportation-related deaths and 99 percent of all transportation-related injuries. They are the leading cause of death for Americans for every age from 3 through 33. Although we are seeing improvements in vehicle crash worthiness and crash avoidance technologies, the numbers of fatalities and injuries on our highways remain staggering. In 2003, the last year for which we have complete data, an estimated 42,643 people were killed in motor vehicle crashes. This number represents a slight decrease of 362 fatalities from 2002 (43,005), but we need to continue and accelerate that downward trend.

A Serious Problem

The economic costs associated with these crashes seriously impact the Nation's fiscal health. The annual cost to our economy of all motor vehicle crashes is $230.6 billion in Year 2000 dollars, or 2.3 percent of the U.S. gross domestic product. This translates into an average of $820 for every person living in the United States. Included in this figure is $81 billion in lost productivity, $32.6 billion in medical expenses, and $59 billion in property damage. The average cost to care for a critically injured survivor is estimated at $1.1 million over a lifetime, a figure that does not begin to account for the physical and psychological suffering of the victims and their families. . . .

As the statistics indicate, traffic safety constitutes a major public health problem. But unlike a number of the complex issues facing the Nation today, we have at least one highly effective and simple remedy to combat highway deaths and injuries. Wearing safety belts is the single most effective step individuals can take to save their lives. Buckling up is not a complex vaccine, doesn't have unwanted side effects and doesn't cost any money. It's simple, it works and it's lifesaving.

Lifesaving Benefits of Seat Belts

Safety belt use cuts the risk of death in a severe crash in half. Most passenger vehicle occupants killed in motor vehicle crashes are unrestrained. If safety belt use were to increase from the 2004 national average of 80 percent to 90 percent—an achievable goal—nearly 2,700 lives would be saved each year. For every 1 percentage point increase in safety belt use—that is 2.8 million more people buckling up—we would save hundreds of lives, suffer significantly fewer injuries, and reduce economic costs by hundreds of millions of dollars a year.

States recognize these lifesaving benefits, and have enacted safety belt laws. However, as of March 2005, only 21 States plus the District of Columbia and Puerto Rico have primary laws, which allow police officers to stop and issue citations to motorists upon observation that they are not buckled up. Other safety belt laws, known as secondary laws, do not allow such citations unless a motorist is stopped for another offense. In 2004, belt use in States with primary safety belt laws averaged 84 percent, 11 points higher than in States with secondary laws—a statistically significant difference. If all States enacted primary safety belt laws, we would prevent 1,275 deaths and 17,000 serious injuries annually. Enacting a primary safety belt law is the single most effective action a State with a secondary law can take to decrease highway deaths and injuries. . . .

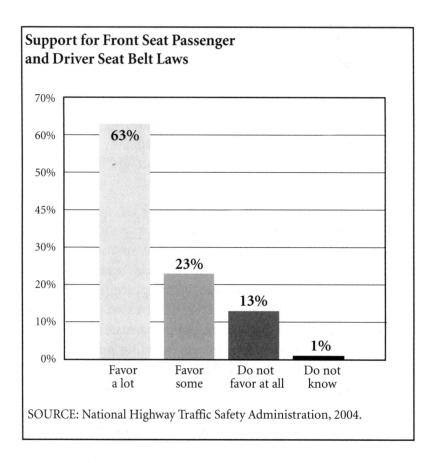

Support for Front Seat Passenger and Driver Seat Belt Laws

SOURCE: National Highway Traffic Safety Administration, 2004.

SAFETEA

The Administration's SAFETEA [Safe, Accountable, Flexible, and Efficient Transportation Equity Act] proposal, transmitted to Congress in 2003 and adjusted this February [2005], proposes . . . a Safety Belt Performance Grant.[1] . . .

The Safety Belt Performance Grant provides up to $100 million each year to reward States for passing primary safety belt laws or achieving 90 percent safety belt use rates in two consecutive years. Under our proposal, a State that has already enacted a primary safety belt use law for all passenger motor vehicles (effective by December 31, 2002) would receive a

1. SAFETEA was signed into law on August 10, 2005.

grant equal to 2.5 times the amount of its FY [fiscal year] 2003 formula grant for highway safety. A State that enacts a new primary belt law or achieves 90 percent belt use for two consecutive years will receive a grant equal to five times the amount of its FY 2003 formula grant for highway safety. This significant incentive is intended to prompt State action needed to save lives. States achieve high levels of belt use through primary safety belt laws, public education using paid and earned media, and high visibility law enforcement programs, such as the *Click it or Ticket* campaign. . . .

Under another provision of the Safety Belt Performance Grant, a State can receive additional grants by improving its safety belt use rates. . . .

Encouraging Enforcement of Seat Belt Laws

These grants reflect a different approach to addressing the Nation's substantial highway safety problems. . . . States . . . should be strongly encouraged to increase their safety belt use rates—the single most effective means of decreasing deaths and injuries—and should be rewarded for performance with increased funds and greater flexibility to spend those funds on either infrastructure safety or behavioral safety programs. . . .

The single most important safety measure Congress could pass this decade is SAFETEA's proposal to provide incentive grants for States to pass primary belt laws. As the Nation's chief highway safety official, I urge you to pass a bill that gives States the strongest incentives possible to enact primary belt laws. No vehicle safety mandate, no elaborate rulemaking, no public relations campaign that NHTSA could undertake would have the lifesaving impact of Congress providing meaningful incentives to the States to pass primary belt laws.

> *"[Enforcement of seat belt laws] distracts law enforcement from more important duties."*

Enforcement of Seat Belt Laws Is a Waste of Resources

Ted Balaker

While there is overwhelming evidence that seat belt laws save lives, the government should not make laws penalizing drivers who do not buckle up, Ted Balaker argues in the following viewpoint. In Balaker's opinion, such laws are an unwarranted violation of Americans' freedom. In addition, he maintains, these laws simply protect careless people from themselves and thus waste public resources. He believes that a better use of police power would be to stop reckless drivers who are truly endangering others. Balaker is a policy analyst and the Jacobs Fellow at the Reason Foundation, a nonprofit think tank.

As you read, consider the following questions:

1. As cited by the author, of the ten safest states, how many had primary seat belt enforcement laws in 2002?
2. According to Balaker, what often happens when an officer is spending time to scold and ticket a person for not wearing a seat belt?

Ted Balaker, "Do Seat Belt Laws Save Lives?" www.reason.org, August 17, 2004. Copyright © 2004 by the Reason Foundation, 3415 S. Sepulveda Blvd., Suite 400, Los Angeles, CA 90034, www.reason.com. Reproduced by permission.

3. In the author's opinion, upon what do most people probably base the decision to buckle up?

W e know that seat belts save lives, but what about seat belt laws?

One year ago [in 2003] Illinois began enforcing a tougher, "primary enforcement" law, which allows cops to pull over those whose only offense is not buckling up. Police officers set up special checkpoints and enforcement zones, and doled out 43,000 more tickets than the previous year. The results: seat belt use is up 9 percent and, most importantly, there were 63 fewer automobile fatalities. Sounds like a success.

A Tenuous Link

But are streets getting safer because of the new law, or has the law simply jumped in front of a long developing social trend? After all, Illinois' streets have been getting safer for a long time. In 1982 there were 2.51 highway fatalities per 100 million vehicle miles traveled. Twenty years later the fatality rate fell to 1.34, an impressive 47 percent drop which preceded the new law.

Most states have enjoyed progressively safer streets, often regardless of the harshness of their seat belt laws. In 2002, of the 10 safest states, five had primary enforcement laws and five did not. Of the top five, only one had primary enforcement. And New Hampshire, the only state with no seat belt law, had the nation's third safest streets. In other words, the link between tough seat belt laws and lives saved is more tenuous than politicians let on.

Protecting the Wrong People

So why waste cops' time with seat belt laws? After all, laws shouldn't protect careless people from themselves, they should protect the peaceful from the dangerous.

If an adult does something risky—like tightrope walking, smoking or driving without a seat belt—that person alone is

No One's Business

What business is it of the police if I don't wear a seat belt? If I'm in an accident and am not wearing a seat belt, the only one I injure is me. My not wearing a seat belt infringes on no one else's rights, which brings up the only legitimate function of the law and the police, to stop or arrest those who infringe on the rights of others, like rapists, thieves, and murderers.

Alexander Marriott, Capitalism Magazine, *December 28, 2003.*

responsible for the consequences. And since drivers who don't buckle up aren't making anyone else less safe, laws that bear down on these people don't make other motorists any safer either. Yes it's tragic when someone dies because he refused to wear a seat belt, but it's much more tragic when a reckless driver kills innocent people.

Some of us decry the paternalism of seat belt laws, but such nannying doesn't just make us less free. If it distracts law enforcement from more important duties, it can also make us less safe. When government assumes many duties, it's tougher to do the important ones right.

Misuse of Resources

While an officer takes time to give the seat belt scofflaw a scolding and a ticket, plenty of other drivers embark on the kind of harebrained maneuvering that often ends with a reckless driver colliding into a good driver. It's these red-light-running, left-turn-at-any-cost daredevils who enrage and endanger good drivers.

Officials are more on the mark when they call for enforcement of drunk driving laws. But here again law should focus on recklessness, whether it's encouraged by alcohol, fatigue, or high-speed lipstick application.

So is Illinois truly better off for having issued 43,000 more seat belt tickets or would the effort spent on seat belt checkpoints and enforcement zones been better spent protecting good drivers from bad?

No Excuse for Nannying

Some argue that seat belt laws do benefit good drivers—for those who refuse to belt themselves in may stick the rest of us with higher insurance and health care costs. But excusing nannying on such grounds would excuse all sorts of awfulness. Those who eat too much and move too little cost our nation much more than those who refuse to buckle up, yet most of us would consider it absurd if laws forced chubby people away from the fridge and onto the treadmill.

The good news is that most people do buckle up. In Illinois, about 83 percent of motorists use seat belts, a decision probably based less on government nagging and more on a simple understanding of the safety benefits. After all, the word is out—seat belts make you safer. Why wage an ever-intensifying campaign against the remaining holdouts?

We must accept that—even when armed with all the facts—some people will still choose risky behavior. Instead of saving us from ourselves, regulators should take a deep breath, allow beltless motorists to put themselves at risk, and go hassle the dangerous drivers.

> "It's certainly been found that when countries lower their [blood alcohol content] limits there are fewer crashes. . . . Everybody drinks and drives less."

America Needs Stricter Drunk Driving Laws

John Valenti

Compared to other countries, the United States has very lenient drunk driving laws, states John Valenti in the following viewpoint. He believes these lax laws are the cause of many drunk driving accidents in America. According to Valenti, countries with strict drunk driving penalties have a far lower incidence of accidents than does the United States. He believes America should lower the blood alcohol standard and strictly enforce the new law. Valenti is a columnist for Newsday, *a daily online and print newspaper.*

As you read, consider the following questions:

1. As cited by the author, what is the blood alcohol concentration standard in the United States?

2. According to Valenti, can police in the United States stop any motorist at any time and make him or her submit to a breath test?

3. By how much did Belgium's drunk driving fatalities decline the year after it tightened its blood alcohol content standards, according to the author?

I f you go to a party in Sweden, it's perfectly acceptable to drink. But you'd better not drive—not even after one beer.

The standard for drunken driving in Sweden is .02 percent blood-alcohol concentration—the equivalent of one 12-ounce beer, one 1.5-ounce shot of hard liquor or one 5-ounce glass of wine in one hour.

It is a standard far stricter than ours of .08 percent.

And in Japan, where the standard is .03 percent blood-alcohol content—but zero tolerance in the practical sense—a driver can be arrested and charged with DWI [driving while intoxicated] after having just a few sips of alcohol.

"A sip of beer, a sip of wine," said Tamotsu Ide, a former Japanese police captain and Chief of Security for the Consulate General of Japan in New York. "It's almost impossible to drive after even that much. . . . Any drink, you will get caught."

Despite great strides in awareness, education and enforcement in the last two decades, the United States still has one of the most lenient drunken-driving standards in the world, according to the National Highway Traffic Safety Administration [NHTSA].

But, in the wake of a horrific crash like the one recently on the Meadowbrook Parkway, where police said a wrong-way drunken driver killed a limousine driver and a 7-year-old flower girl, experts said we can learn a lot from how other countries combat drunk driving.

"We're at a much lower level [of DWI offenses] than we were 20 years ago," said Kathryn Stewart, chairwoman of the National Academy of Sciences Committee on Alcohol, Other Drugs and Transportation and the author of a NHTSA study on DWI laws in other countries. "But we still have one of the highest BAC [blood-alcohol content] limits in the world."

Blood Alcohol Concentration at Which Drivers Are Legally Drunk

BAC: 0.00

Country: Czech Republic, Slovakia, Hungary

BAC: 0.02

Country: Norway, Poland, Sweden

BAC: 0.03

Country: Japan, China

BAC: 0.05

Country: Argentina, Australia, Costa Rica, Denmark, Finland, France, Italy, Germany, Greece, Netherlands, Peru, Russia, South Africa, Spain, Thailand

BAC: 0.08

Country: Brazil, Britain, Canada, Chile, Ecuador, Ireland, Jamaica, New Zealand, Singapore, United States

NOTE: The average male would have to have four drinks (a 12-ounce beer, 1.5 ounces of hard liquor, 5 ounces of wine) to reach a 0.08 BAC

John Valenti, Newsday, *July 13, 2005.*

A significant number of countries have a DWI standard of .05 percent blood-alcohol content, including Australia and at least 10 European nations.

The standard is even less in China and Norway. It is absolutely zero in the Czech Republic and Slovakia.

"It's so widely accepted that it is a serious crime to drive under the influence that people don't," said Amelie Heinsjo, spokeswoman for the Consulate General of Sweden in New York. "If you have a drink and try to drive, people will raise an eyebrow."

And, she said, there is a good chance you will be caught.

Many countries use random breath testing to enforce these tough standards. Police in Sweden and Australia, for instance, can stop any motorist anywhere at any time and make them submit to a breath test—without probable cause. Police in this country cannot do that.

In her study, Stewart found that, in the Australian state of Victoria, where more than 2.4 million drivers are stopped for random breath tests annually, a first offense carries a maximum fine of 180,000 Australian dollars—about $135,000 in American currency. The fear factor keeps most drivers from driving drunk.

A first offender in Belgium who registers more than .08 percent blood-alcohol content faces a fine of 400,000 Belgian francs—about $12,000—and a second offense within three years can earn a fine of 1 million francs—more than $30,000—with that fine doubled for yet another offense in three years.

Any wonder there was a 14-percent reduction in drunken-driving fatalities in Belgium in 1995, the year after it tightened its standard to .05 percent blood-alcohol content?

The Swedes use alkolas—an ignition interlock system—to prevent drunken driving by convicted offenders.

These methods work, Stewart said. And Stewart found drivers often do not mind the intrusions. For instance, drivers in Finland actually favor a legal limit of zero.

They don't want drunken drivers on their roads.

"It's certainly been found," Stewart said, "that when countries lower their limits there are fewer crashes. . . . Everybody drinks and drives less."

"*[Drunk driving] laws should be grounded in sound science and the presumption of innocence, not in hysteria.*"

America's Drunk Driving Laws Are Too Strict

Radley Balko

In the following viewpoint Radley Balko argues that America's drunk driving laws are unconstitutional. He maintains that these laws violate the civil liberties of Americans by mandating blood testing and presuming guilt before proven. Moreover, current laws are based on an incorrect estimation of alcohol-related fatalities that exaggerate the drunk driving problem, claims Balko. Balko is a policy analyst for the Cato Institute, a nonprofit public policy research foundation.

As you read, consider the following questions:

1. According to the *Los Angeles Times* in 2002, of eighteen thousand alcohol related fatalities, how many actually involved a drunk driver taking the life of a sober driver, pedestrian, or passenger?

2. How many states reserve the right to revoke drunken driving defendants' licenses before they are brought to trial, according to Balko?

3. What law did New Mexico's state legislature recently attempt to pass, as explained by the author?

When Pennsylvanian Keith Emerich went to the hospital recently for an irregular heartbeat, he told his doctor he was a heavy drinker: a six-pack per day. Later, Pennsylvania's Department of Transportation sent Emerich a letter. His driver's license had been revoked. If Emerich wanted it back, he'd need to prove to Pennsylvania authorities that he was competent to drive. His doctor had turned him in, as required by state law.

Infringing on Civil Liberties

The Pennsylvania law is old (it dates back to the 1960s), but it's hardly unusual. Courts and lawmakers have stripped DWI [driving while intoxicated] defendants of the presumption of innocence—along with several other common criminal justice protections we afford to the likes of accused rapists, murderers and pedophiles.

In the 1990 case *Michigan v. Sitz*, the U.S. Supreme Court ruled that the magnitude of the drunken driving problem outweighed the "slight" intrusion into motorists' protections against unreasonable search effected by roadblock sobriety checkpoints. Writing for the majority, Chief Justice [William] Rehnquist ruled that the 25,000 roadway deaths due to alcohol were reason enough to set aside the Fourth Amendment.

The problem is that the 25,000 number was awfully misleading. It included any highway fatality in which alcohol was in any way involved: a sober motorist striking an intoxicated pedestrian, for example.

It's a number that's still used today. In 2002, the *Los Angeles Times* examined accident data and estimated that in the previous year, of the 18,000 "alcohol-related" traffic fatalities drunk driving activists cited the year before, only about 5,000 involved a drunk driver taking the life of a sober driver, pedestrian, or passenger.

Unreliable Statistics

NHTSA [National Highway Traffic Safety Administration] can no longer be considered an impartial arbiter of the nation's accident statistics. Its oft-quoted statistic that drunk driving took 17,448 lives in 2001 is based on flawed initial reporting, questionable computer simulations, and outright misrepresentation. The *Los Angeles Times* tells the story of an Alabama State Trooper named Darrick Dorough who was assigned to investigate a fatal crash. Dorough reported that the driver had been drinking, but he never took an alcohol test, and he later could not recall why he suspected drinking in the first place: "I don't think drinking was the primary cause of the accident. It could have contributed to it. That's a guess." Still, NHTSA labeled that "guess" as an alcohol-related fatality. Such are the stories that comprise NHTSA's statistics.

Then there are the cases where no one even reported alcohol usage. NHTSA uses a mathematical model to determine whether some crashes involved alcohol. According to the *LA Times*, "If a young man hits a tree early in the morning, the model would classify the crash as alcohol-related, even without any evidence of alcohol."

Charles V. Peña, "The Anti–Drunk
Driving Campaign: A Covert War
Against Drinking," n.d.

Unfortunately, courts and legislatures still regularly cite the inflated "alcohol-related" number when justifying new laws that chip away at our civil liberties.

Unreasonable Laws

For example, the Supreme Court has ruled that states may legislate away a motorist's Sixth Amendment right to a jury trial and his Fifth Amendment right against self-incrimination.

In 2002, the Supreme Court of Wisconsin ruled that police officers could forcibly extract blood from anyone suspected of drunk driving. Other courts have ruled that prosecutors aren't obligated to provide defendants with blood or breath test samples for independent testing (even though both are feasible and relatively cheap to do). In almost every other facet of criminal law, defendants are given access to the evidence against them.

These decisions haven't gone unnoticed in state legislatures. Forty-one states now reserve the right to revoke drunken driving defendants' licenses before they're ever brought to trial. Thirty-seven states now impose *harsher* penalties on motorists who refuse to take roadside sobriety tests than on those who take them and fail. Seventeen states have laws denying drunk driving defendants the same opportunities to plea bargain given to those accused of violent crimes.

Until recently, New York City cops could seize the cars of first-offender drunk driving suspects upon arrest. Those acquitted or otherwise cleared of charges were still required to file civil suits to get their cars back, which typically cost thousands of dollars. The city of Los Angeles still seizes the cars of suspected first-time drunk drivers, as well as the cars of those suspected of drug activity and soliciting prostitutes.

Newer laws are even worse. As of last month [June 2004], Washington State now requires anyone arrested (not convicted—*arrested*) for drunken driving to install an "ignition interlock" device, which forces the driver to blow into a breath test tube before starting the car, and at regular intervals while driving. A second law mandates that juries hear all drunken driving cases. It then instructs juries to consider the evidence *"in a light most favorable to the prosecution,"* [an] absurd evidentiary standard at odds with everything the American criminal justice system is supposed to stand for.

The Wrong Way to Address Drunk Driving

Even scarier are the laws that didn't pass, but will inevitably be introduced again. New Mexico's state legislature nearly passed a law that would mandate ignition interlock devices on every car sold in the state beginning in 2008, regardless of the buyer's driving record. Drivers would have been required to pass a breath test to start the car, then again every 10 minutes while driving. Car computer systems would have kept records of the tests, which would have been downloaded at service centers and sent to law enforcement officials for evaluation. New York considered a similar law.

That isn't to say we ought to ease up on drunken drivers. But our laws should be grounded in sound science and the presumption of innocence, not in hysteria. They should target repeat offenders and severely impaired drunks, not social drinkers who straddle the legal threshold. Though the threat of drunken driving has significantly diminished over the last 20 years, it's still routinely overstated by anti-alcohol activists and lawmakers. Even if the threat were as severe as it's often portrayed, casting aside basic criminal protections and civil liberties is the wrong way to address it.

"If there were a drug as effective [as the black box] in saving lives, people would be clamoring outside the Food & Drug Administration for its approval."

Black Boxes for Cars

Ian Ayres and Barry Nalebuff

Installing black boxes in cars can make driving safer, assert Ian Ayres and Barry Nalebuff in the following viewpoint. First, they point out, black boxes allow investigators to determine what caused a fatal accident, helping them to prevent such crashes from happening again. Second, argue Ayres and Nalebuff, because black boxes record everything a driver does, they may motivate unsafe drivers to change their behavior out of fear of being caught. Parents could install the devices on teens' cars, and insurance companies could require that their policyholders use them. Ayres is Townsend Professor at Yale Law School and Nalebuff is Steinbach Professor at Yale School of Management.

As you read, consider the following questions:

1. According to Ayres and Nalebuff, by how much did taxi collision rates fall in Germany after black boxes were installed in the fleet?

2. What may be a more powerful motivator than fear of getting killed, in the authors' opinion?

Ian Ayres and Barry Nalebuff, "Black Boxes for Cars," *Forbes*, vol. 171, August 11, 2003, p. 84. Copyright © 2003 by Forbes, Inc. Reprinted by permission.

3. Why is the privacy of teenagers not a concern when it comes to driving, as argued by Ayres and Nalebuff?

W hen we started this column last year, FORBES challenged us to report back if any why-not ideas make it to the product shelf. Road Safety International offers an inspiring example of bringing a why-not idea to market. Driving a car is one of the most dangerous things people do. There are 24 million auto accidents a year, and 2.4 million people are injured in them. Annually, the number of auto fatalities would be equivalent to the deaths from a 737 plane crash every day.

Most of us don't want to think about the dangers of driving. That fatalistic attitude is wrong. It's possible to make automobiles safer and make money in the process. To see how, take a lesson from airplanes. The first thing people do after a plane crash is look for the "black box" (more formally known as the event data recorder). Why not a black box for cars? It would allow police and carmakers to understand what happened just before the crash. The traditional way of reconstructing events, looking at skid marks and steel deformation, is extremely unreliable.

The National Highway Traffic Safety Administration (NHTSA) determined this while investigating a fatal accident that, based on the skid marks and appearance of the bent steel, appeared to have occurred at 23 miles per hour. Was there a design flaw? General Motors let the investigators know that the car had stored its speed at the time of crash. The estimate was off by more than a factor of two. The car was doing 50mph.

Remember the scare about sudden acceleration in Audis? With event data recorders, we would have known from the beginning that the drivers had their feet on the accelerator, not the brake. How about the Ford Explorer rollovers? We would know what the g-forces were at the time of an accident.

Helping Crash Investigators

In recent years car crashes have become increasingly difficult to reconstruct because of advances such as anti-lock
brakes, which prevent wheels locking and leaving telltale
skid marks from which investigators can estimate speed.
"Every new generation of cars makes the problem bigger,"
says Ad Hellemons, director of European affairs for the
Dutch police and president of the European Traffic Police
Network (TISPOL). The black box data is a godsend for
crash investigators.

James Randerson, New Scientist, *January 10, 2004.*

It isn't only that black boxes can make cars safer. They can
also make safer drivers. The Berlin highway safety administration found that after the city's police department started using
data recorders in their patrol cars, damage during rescue trips
fell by 36%. Also in Germany, a taxi company installed these
boxes in its fleet and collision rates fell by 66%. In the U.S.,
Sunstar Emergency Medical Services found that black boxes
reduced its ambulance accidents by 95%. If there were a drug
as effective in saving lives, people would be clamoring outside
the Food & Drug Administration for its approval.

Just knowing the box is there changes drivers' behavior.
Fear of getting caught may be a more powerful motivator
than fear of getting killed. Better still, these devices give real-
time feedback to drivers when they are doing something dangerous. Ricardo Martinez, the former head of the NHTSA, re-
members his days working ambulances in Louisiana. The
vehicles had something called a Growler. If he accelerated too
fast or took a corner too hard, the machine would squawk. If
he didn't slow down, it would squawk louder and make a
record of the transgression. When he got back to base, he'd

have to explain the indicators. The Growler made him drive more safely.

Larry H. Selditz, owner of Road Safety, a ten-year-old firm in Thousand Oaks, Calif., has taken the idea and made it available for the family car. As he points out, teenagers drive much better when their parents are sitting next to them. His black box device is always there watching the driver. When the kids come home, the parents can download driving information to review.

Road Safety has sold some 10,000 black boxes (at $4,000 a shot) to operators of ambulances, squad cars and other high-risk vehicles. On Sept. 8 the firm will launch a $280 consumer version. It won't have all the furbelows, but it will report on safety-belt use, acceleration/deceleration and four other measures of potentially unsafe driving.

For teenagers (and their parents) there are two large costs associated with having a new driver in the family. Insurance premiums go through the roof. And parents lie awake at 1 a.m. wondering if they will get a call from an emergency room.

Some people are worried about privacy. We're not. If our teenagers are concerned about privacy, they can get their own cars and buy their own insurance.

The privacy issue becomes more serious when insurance companies come into play. But, even here, the system gives warnings. Thus drivers can correct their behavior before any black marks are recorded. You can bet that there will be a careful-driver discount given to people who agree to install a black box. Insurance companies are lining up to distribute Road Safety's product. Soon people who drive more responsibly (and wear safety belts) will be able to buy insurance at a discount. Perhaps GM will use its existing technology to create a rival product. Stay tuned.

"Consumers, not the government, should decide if they want their cars to collect ... data [on their driving habits], and if they want to share it with others."

Black Boxes in Cars Threaten Civil Liberties

Jim Harper

In the following viewpoint Jim Harper argues that while black boxes might be a valuable tool in improving automobile safety, they also pose a serious threat to civil liberties. According to Harper, black boxes, also called Event Data Recorders, are often used without drivers' knowledge or consent. He believes such surveillance is unconstitutional, and contends that drivers should be allowed to decide whether or not they want their driving habits monitored by a black box. Harper is director of information policy studies at the Cato Institute, a nonprofit public policy research foundation.

As you read, consider the following questions:

1. How many 2004 cars and light vehicles have some type of recording capability, according to Harper?
2. As explained by the author, what evidence was used to convict Robert Christmann in a traffic fatality?
3. According to Harper, how did a Connecticut car rental company use black boxes in 2001?

New cars offer a delightful array of information and services: satellite radio, intelligent cruise control, braking and steering assistance, navigation systems, and roadside assistance, to name a few. These all appeal to drivers' desire for safety, convenience, and comfort.

The Black Box

But a troublesome feature of most new cars is the Event Data Recorder ("EDR"), or Black Box. As in commercial airplanes, the automobile Black Box keeps a running record of how a car is being operated, including speed, acceleration, braking, steering, and seat belt use.

When there is an "event"—usually a crash—the EDR moves the last several seconds of information into long-term storage for later downloading. Well over half of the 2004 model passenger cars and light vehicles have some recording capability of this type.

The National Highway Traffic Safety Administration has proposed standards for the data collected by EDRs, but the agency emphasized in a notice that it is not mandating Black Boxes. It will be under pressure to do so. The National Transportation Safety Board has listed Black Boxes as one of its "most wanted" measures.

There are obvious safety benefits if auto accidents can be dissected in detail, of course. Auto manufacturers, safety groups, and insurers want this information. Police departments want it too.

Already, prosecutors are using information from automobile Black Boxes as evidence against drivers. Last year [2003], one Robert Christmann was convicted in a New York traffic fatality based upon information downloaded from his car's Black Box.

Misinterpreting the Data

Some safety experts . . . worry about the wrong people using the data [from black boxes]. While Mr. [Joe] Osterman of the NTSB [National Transportation Safety Board] favors police investigators using black-box data in criminal investigations, he worries that private experts hired in civil litigation may have biases and could take the data at face value instead of cross-checking it.

"The data can be misleading if you're not a seasoned accident reconstructionist," adds Bob Kreeb, an engineer at Booz Allen Hamilton in Washington who chaired a committee of the Society of Automotive Engineers to set standards for the data gathered from black boxes. "So it needs to be interpreted and validated."

Eric C. Evarts, USA Today, *December 27, 2004.*

A Surveillance Tool

But car manufacturers aren't touting the safety benefits of the Black Box like they do so many other improvements on the modern automobile. That is because the Black Box is not a safety feature; it is a surveillance tool—and when drivers learn about it, they are none too happy.

After I commented on Black Boxes in a news story earlier this year [2004], letters poured into my e-mail box. "This is 'over the top,' and a definite infringement on my privacy," said one outraged car owner. Another wrote, "This is a personal vehicle, I've paid for it, paid my taxes, enough said." From another, simply: "Not on my car."

Many correspondents wanted to know which cars have Black Boxes so they can determine whether their personal vehicles were, in effect, spying on them.

The Future of Black Boxes

There are a number of directions in which this technology is likely to go. It could collect and retain more information for longer periods. It could interact with Global Positioning Systems (GPS) to record where a car has traveled. And it could combine with communications systems to signal authorities in real time.

Joan Borucki, Governor Arnold Schwarzenegger's nominee to head California's Department of Motor Vehicles, has proposed a mileage tax that Black Boxes could administer. The Oregon Department of Transportation has also considered a mileage tax.

In 2001, a Connecticut car rental company began charging renters a $150 fine for speeding in their rental cars, using a GPS-equipped monitoring system. Consumers can shun companies which make this a practice. But they could not refuse an automatically-issued traffic citation if governments were to add Black-Box-citation revenue to what they now get from red-light cameras.

Legislation passed by the state of California is likely a sign where things are headed. The state requires notices in the owner's manuals of cars that have Black Boxes. The new law also allows data to be accessed under court order, for research, and for other reasons. California's EDR law replaced consumer choice with an agreement among politicians, bureaucrats, and industry on a nice low level of protection for consumers.

Consumers Should Decide

There is no question that aggregated EDR data can provide important safety benefits. If traffic accidents and deaths can be averted by improving automobile safety, these safety advances should be pursued. But they should be pursued in a way that unites the interests of drivers with the interests of the community.

Insurers should offer car owners discounts if their EDR-equipped cars reveal good driving habits and freedom from blame in accidents. Consumers, not the government, should decide if they want their cars to collect such data, and if they want to share it with others.

| "SUVs are less safe on average for their occupants . . . and yet inflict far greater costs in both lives and money on other motorists."

Sport Utility Vehicles Make Driving Unsafe

Joan Claybrook

According to the congressional testimony of Joan Claybrook in the following viewpoint, sport utility vehicles (SUVs) endanger both their occupants and other drivers on the road. Despite the claims of some, SUVs are not safer for occupants than are passenger cars, says Claybrook, and they actually contribute to a high number of fatalities because of their likelihood to roll over. In addition, she maintains, because of their size and construction, SUVs destroy passenger cars in crashes. She criticizes car manufacturers for knowing about these dangers yet continuing to manufacture and market these cars to consumers. Claybrook is president of Public Citizen, a consumer advocacy organization, and former administrator of the National Highway Traffic Safety Administration.

As you read, consider the following questions:

1. As cited by the author, between 1995 and 2001, what was the rate of decline in fatal crashes for passenger cars compared to light trucks?

Joan Claybrook, testimony before the U.S. Senate Committee on Commerce, Science, and Transportation, Washington, DC, February 26, 2003.

2. According to Claybrook, what percentage of SUV occupant fatalities are due to rollovers?

3. Why is it impossible that the SUV market reflects a true social need, as argued by the author?

C riticism of SUVs [sport utility vehicles] is richly deserved. SUVs are basically gussied-up pickup trucks, and most have never been comprehensively re-designed to be safely used as passenger vehicles. In a crash, the high bumper, stiff frame and steel-panel construction of SUVs override crash protections of other vehicles. Due to their cut-rate safety design, SUVs often fail to adequately absorb crash energy or to crumple as they should, so they ram into other motorists and shock their own occupants' bodies. Endangering their occupants, SUVs may also slide over roadside guardrails, which were designed for cars. And their high profile and narrow track width create a tippy vehicle, which, when combined with their weak roofs and poor crash protection, places SUV drivers at risk of death or paralysis in a devastating rollover crash. All of these factors mean that overall, SUVs are less safe on average for their occupants than large or mid-size cars, and yet inflict far greater costs in both lives and money on other motorists.

Ignoring the Carnage

The SUV is a bad bargain for society and a nightmare for American roads. The switch from mid-size and large passenger cars to SUVs has endangered millions of Americans, without any recognizable benefits. One former NHTSA [National Highway Traffic Safety Administration] Administrator estimated in 1997 that the aggressive design of light trucks (a category including SUVs, pickup trucks, vans and minivans) has killed 2,000 additional people needlessly each year. Yet automakers continue to exploit special interest exemptions and safety loopholes, while creating consumer demand and shaping consumer choice with a multibillion-dollar marketing campaign, because SUVs bring in maximum dollars for minimal effort.

After years of losing out in the passenger car market to foreign manufacturers, the domestics' decision to produce and market vehicles in the far less regulated, tariff-protected SUV category was like hitting the lottery for Detroit. In the SUV, the industry found and developed a broad market that allowed it to rake in cash, while taking every step to avoid spending money to fix the unstable and threatening vehicle that resulted.

Manufacturers have known for decades about the tendency of SUVs to roll over, and about the damage incurred when the vehicles' weak roof crushes in on the heads and spines of motorists. Manufacturers have settled the many lawsuits brought by motorists who were horribly injured by these vehicles and facing a lifetime of pain, often imposing gag orders to hide the documents that show this knowledge. They've also unblinkingly faced the carnage inflicted on other motorists from high SUV bumpers and menacing front grilles, building ever-more heavy and terrible SUVs over time and continuing to market them militaristically, such as the ads calling the Lincoln Navigator an "urban assault vehicle." For this designed-in harm, they are rarely held responsible. Throughout, they've kept churning out millions of SUVs, essentially unfixed. . . .

Better regulation is sorely needed to transform this socially and environmentally hostile vehicle into one worth selling or owning.

A Growing Death Toll

Although many Americans purchase SUVs because they believe that they will safely transport their families, the truth is that SUVs are among the most dangerous vehicles on the road. They are no more safe for their drivers than many passenger cars, and are much more dangerous for other drivers who share the highway, making them a net social loss for society. Yet this cycle is perpetuated by industry-spread myths that heavier vehicles are safer *per se*, so consumers believe that they must continue to "super-size" their own vehicle in order to remain safe. The self-reinforcing nature of this growing highway arms race makes the notion that SUVs are safe for their occupants one of the more harmful myths of our time.

Yet the influx of these new urban assault vehicles is threatening overall road safety in new and more frightening ways. While the rate of passenger cars involved in fatal crashes per 100,000 registered passenger cars declined by 15.1 percent between 1995 and 2001, the rate of light truck involvement only declined only by 6.8 percent during the same time. Thus, while light truck involvement rates in fatal crashes have always been greater than those of passenger cars, this difference is growing ever larger.

The growing death toll from SUVs is so significant that a recent federal study found that fatalities in rollover crashes in light trucks, a category which includes SUVs, threatens to overwhelm *all other reductions in fatalities on the highway*, an astonishing fact when we consider that air bags are now a requirement for new vehicles and seat belt use keeps going up. NHTSA explained that "the increase in light truck occupant fatalities accounts for the continued high level of overall occupant fatalities, *having offset the decline in traffic deaths of passenger car occupants*." In addition to the height of the vehicles' profiles and headlamps, which block sightlines on the highway, light truck design is so incompatible with passenger vehicles that they are estimated to kill approximately 2,000 unnecessary vehicle occupants each year, as noted by a previous NHTSA Administrator. A more specific analysis found that 1,434 passenger car drivers who were killed in collisions with light trucks would have lived if they had been hit instead by a passenger car of the same weight as the light truck, even under the same crash conditions. The deadly design of light

'I'm sorry — I just didn't see you.'

Nicholas. © 1991 by *The Spectator.* Reproduced by permission.

trucks has thus been responsible for thousands of unnecessary deaths on American highways.

No Safer for Drivers

Overall, SUVs are no safer for their occupants than are many passenger cars. NHTSA's fatality statistics show that, in 2001, there were 162 deaths per million SUVs and 157 deaths per million cars, indicating that the death rate for SUVs is slightly higher. In fact, researchers Marc Ross, of the University of Michigan, and Tom Wenzel, of Lawrence Berkley National Laboratory, have examined detailed crash data and concluded that risks to drivers of SUVs are slightly higher than risks to drivers of mid-size and large cars, but slightly lower than risks to drivers of compact and subcompact cars. When the risk to drivers is combined with the risk to drivers of other vehicles, the average SUV has about the same combined risk as the average compact car (and higher combined risk than average mid-size and large cars, while lower combined risk than the average subcompact). . . .

Rollover Accidents

SUVs are a major part of the rollover problem: while 22 percent of passenger car occupant fatalities are attributable to rollover, a whopping 61 percent of SUV occupant fatalities are. The high frame and unstable design of SUVs makes SUV rollovers particularly likely, and the weak roofs and poor crash protection make them deadly when they do occur. SUV rollovers are dangerous no matter how you slice the data:

- *High overall death toll from SUV rollovers* : SUV rollovers resulted in 12,000 deaths in the U.S. in the 1990s and increased from 2,064 in 2000 to 2,142 in 2001. According to the NHTSA Administrator, in 2001, SUV occupants were far more likely to die in fatal rollover crashes than were other vehicle occupants. SUV occupant fatalities in rollover crashes occurred at a rate of 9.9 per 100,000 registered vehicles, compared to a rate of 3.53 for passenger cars, 4.33 for vans, and 6.97 for pickup trucks.

- *High SUV involvement in fatal rollovers* : According to NHTSA, the rate at which SUVs roll over in fatal crashes is more than three times the rate of passenger cars. While passenger cars roll over in fatal crashes at a rate of 3.48 per 100,000 registered vehicles, SUVs roll over at a rate of 11.06, pickups roll over at a rate of 7.52, and vans roll over at a rate of 4.09.

- *High rate of SUV rollover fatal crashes* : While the rate of passenger car occupants who died in fatal rollover crashes per 100,000 registered vehicles declined 9.7 percent between 1995 and 1999, the rate for SUV occupants declined only 1.8 percent in the same time period.

Critically, SUV occupant death rate in rollover crashes has remained about three times that of passenger car occupant deaths.

And the problem is growing. The rate of passenger car occupants who died in fatal rollover crashes per 100,000 registered vehicles declined 18.5 percent between 1991 and 2000, while the rate of light truck occupants who died in fatal rollover crashes increased 36 percent between 1991 and 2000....

Not a Consumer Necessity

Although manufacturers claim consumer choice drives the light truck market, they spend billions each year to both create and enlarge these consumer preferences. The auto industry spends more per year on advertising than any other industry in the United States, and more than the next three biggest spenders (financial services, telecommunications, and national restaurant chains) combined. SUV advertising, in particular, has grown to exorbitant levels in the past decade, exceeding in percentages even the growth of SUV sales. In 1990, manufacturers spent $172.5 million on SUV advertising, and in 2000 they spent an incredible $1.51 billion. Over the last decade, manufacturers spent over $9 billion to advertise their highly profitable SUV.

Automakers have made a huge financial investment in an attempt to persuade consumers to purchase SUVs. Yet the argument that the market for SUVs somehow correlates to a real economic demand would be laughable if it were not so frequently rehearsed by automakers. Despite being marketed to consumers as rugged, go-anywhere vehicles, only a small percentage of SUVs are actually used for their off-road and towing abilities. SUVs are, instead, an expensive fantasy packaged up for America by Detroit—an "off-road luxury" vehicle marketed primarily to suburbanites with little need for these features and little awareness of the safety risks. Detroit's fantastical images of trucks marauding through empty moun-tainscapes bear so little resemblance to the vehicle's typical use that it is patently implausible that the SUV market reflects a true social need. . . .

A Shocking Toll

In addition the shocking toll in lives, devastating injuries, and unnecessary suffering, the monetary costs of our failure to regulate SUVs is staggering. NHTSA estimates the "compre-hensive cost" of each motor vehicle crash fatality in FY 2000 at approximately $3.4 million. Without adjusting for inflation, the cost to society of SUV rollover fatalities in FY 2001 alone cost the United States approximately $7.3 billion, and has to-taled a shocking 44 billion since 1994. . . . The 2,000 unneces-sary deaths resulting from the aggressivity of light trucks cost the U.S. economy approximately $6.8 billion per year.

8

"Despite alarmist reportage by the major media and SUV-haters ... [SUV rollover accidents are] still pretty low."

The Danger of Sport Utility Vehicles Has Been Exaggerated

Amy Ridenour and Eric Peters

Claims about the dangers associated with sport utility vehicles (SUVs) have been greatly exaggerated by the media and SUV-haters, maintain Amy Ridenour and Eric Peters in the following viewpoint. According to Ridenour and Peters, the number of SUVs involved in rollover crashes is relatively small. In reality, they claim, SUV drivers are usually safer in collisions than are the drivers of typical passenger cars. Of the SUV-related accidents that do occur, the cause is usually not vehicle construction, but a lack of understanding about how to drive the SUV appropriately, argue the authors. Ridenour is president and Peters is a senior fellow of the National Center for Public Policy Research, a Washington, D.C., think tank.

As you read, consider the following questions:

1. As argued by Ridenour and Peters, why does it stand to reason that there have been a greater number of SUV accidents in recent years?
2. What percentage of SUV owners ever take their

Amy Ridenour and Eric Peters, "Rolling Over the Facts on SUV Safety," *National Policy Analysis*, vol. 465, June 2003. Copyright © 2003 by the National Center for Public Policy Research. Reproduced by permission.

SUVs off-road, according to the authors?

3. What types of driving maneuvers can be dangerous in an SUV, as explained by Ridenour and Peters?

More people were killed last year [2002] in rollover-type accidents involving pickups and SUVs than in previous years: statistically speaking, about 1.51 deaths per 100 million vehicle miles traveled. But despite alarmist reportage by the major media and SUV-haters in the punditocracy, this is still pretty low by historical standards of 5.5 million deaths per 100 million vehicle miles traveled in the mid-1960s, and 1.75 per 100 million vehicle miles traveled in 1992.

Exaggeration of the Dangers

Moreover, it's rarely mentioned in anti-SUV rants that rollover-type accidents account for just 2.5 percent of all crashes. Or that the actual number of people killed in these kinds of accidents, while impressive-sounding in terms of percentage increase from year to year—up 4.9 percent from 2001 to 2002—actually represents a relatively small number: 10,626 deaths in 2002 vs. 10,130 in 2001, an increase of 496 deaths.

In a nation of 300 million people with some 16.6 million new vehicles sold every year, half of them SUVs and pickups, that's hardly an epidemic of rollover-type crashes. (For comparison: 3,529 people drowned in swimming pool accidents in 1999 alone, according to the Centers for Disease Control.)

There are also vastly more SUVs and pickups on the roads today than ten or 20 years ago, both in terms of actual numbers and as a percentage of the nation's vehicle fleet. In fact, this year SUVs, pickups and other "light truck" sales will constitute a majority of all new vehicle sales.

It stands to reason that the more SUVs there are on the road, the greater the number of accidents involving them there will be.

Few news stories about the supposedly dramatic rise in fatal accidents involving "dangerous" and "unstable" SUVs mention these facts, though—leaving the average American with the false impression that vehicular carnage is at historic high levels—and that SUVs and pickups are far more risky to drive than they really are.

Some Perspective

While no increase in accidents or fatalities of any sort is a good thing, some perspective is clearly in order.

In the 97.5 percent of accidents that are not rollovers, SUVs are safer to be in than the typical passenger car. In side, frontal and rear-end collisions, for example, the typical 4,500-lb. SUV offers as much as two to three times more protection against impact forces than a 3,000-lb. compact/mid-sized sedan. Also, an SUV with four wheel drive is less likely to be involved in an accident in the first place, or suffer loss of control in certain conditions, such as heavy rain or snow. And 59 percent of those killed in SUV rollover accidents, according to the National Highway Traffic Safety Administration, likely would have survived had they been wearing seatbelts.

Viewed in their totality, the facts indicate that SUVs are more than reasonably safe; indeed, when driven responsibly, their overall safety is demonstrably superior to that of the typical compact and mid-sized passenger car.

Understanding SUV Design

Unfortunately, as SUVs have become popular mass-market vehicles, instead of the specialty/"niche" vehicles they once were, more people who don't really understand SUVs or have much respect for what they are built to do and not do are driving them to work every day.

Some buy SUVs because of their rugged looks, higher ride or ability to carry many groceries. But fewer than five percent of all SUV owners ever take their SUVs off-road, according to auto industry surveys.

The Rollover Danger

It is true that SUVs [sport utility vehicles] are more dangerous to be in should they roll over than are most passenger vehicles. But only 3 percent of all accidents involve roll-overs.

If you're driving an SUV and get into an accident, most of the time it will involve hitting (or getting hit by) something. Accordingly, drivers are right not to worry too much about rolling over in their vehicles, particularly because it can be avoided simply by eschewing NASCAR [National Association for Stock Car Auto Racing] racing practices when making sharp turns.

Jerry Taylor, Washington Times, *February 19, 2003.*

Thus we have the problem of a large and growing group of people who buy SUVs—vehicles specifically built to handle rugged, uneven terrain, deep mud, snow, etc.—but who almost never actually use the off-road capability built into these vehicles. Yet the capabilities built into most SUVs to handle off-road conditions are precisely the source of the SUVs' weaknesses, if driven aggressively—and the root cause of the "rollover epidemic."

A higher center of gravity—when the vehicle's mass is well above the ground—can make an SUV more "tipsy," but this only becomes a serious problem if the driver pushes the SUV into corners, makes violent lane changes or turns at high speed. Mud and snow-rated tires such as are typically found on SUVs are great for the conditions they were designed to deal with, but offer less lateral grip if the vehicle is thrown into a hard turn. Weight transfer is another area in which SUVs differ from passenger cars. Under hard braking, acceleration and cornering, an SUV's weight shifts more dramatically, unsettling the vehicle. This can be a particular problem during a tire failure at high speed (70-plus) as occurred during the recent Ford Explorer/Firestone tire debacle.[1]

Many SUV drivers have gotten themselves into trouble by assuming that an exit ramp or bend posted at 35 or 45 miles per hour (mph) is perfectly safe to take at five to ten mph over the posted limit because their car can handle the same curve at that speed with no difficulty. But the car's strengths in cornering are the SUV's weakness—just as the car would be in trouble in deep snow or attempting to cross a stream. However, it's not the SUV's fault when it's pushed beyond its limits and expected to handle a situation it wasn't designed for any more than it's a "design defect" of the average passenger car that it can't scrabble up dirt-covered backwoods trails very well.

Unfair to Blame the Vehicles

Yet the emphasis of an increasingly vocal group of anti-SUV activists is to blame SUVs first, put out incomplete information about their safety record, and demand new regulations— not to urge that SUV drivers be educated to drive their vehicles appropriately and with respect for their built-in limitations in high-speed, fast-cornering situations.

The auto industry is doing some good by building more on-road-friendly SUVs called "crossovers" that are built on car-type platforms that are lower to the ground and which therefore ride, handle and behave more like passenger cars, even though they still look like burly SUVs on the outside.

But there's only so much idiot-proofing that can be done. People who insist on driving their SUVs at 80 mph and weaving through dense traffic—then taking off-ramps posted at 35 mph at 50 mph—are going to get into trouble no matter what the federal government forces the automakers to do.

1. In 2000 a high incidence of tire failure on Ford Explorers fitted with Firestone tires was discovered. Many failures caused rollovers. A product recall was announced, and many lawsuits were filed against both Ford and Firestone.

But it's unfair (and counterproductive) to blame the vehicles and those who build them—or to force responsible SUV drivers to pay more for new technology and equipment, such as factory-installed stability control systems, etc. that are designed to protect the willfully irresponsible from themselves.

Periodical Bibliography

The following articles have been selected to supplement the diverse views presented in this chapter.

Ira Carnahan	"Sober Up," *Forbes*, July 26, 2004.
Bob Gritzinger	"Big Brother Is Riding Shotgun; 20 Years After 1984, Orwell's Novel Is Reality with Our Cars Acting as Spies," *Automotive News*, November 15, 2004.
Danny Hakim	"Safety Gap Grows Wider Between S.U.V.'s and Cars," *New York Times*, August 17, 2004.
Mick Hamer	"How to Stop the Slaughter of Innocents: Cars Could Be Re-Engineered to Make Them Safer for Pedestrians. But Will Car Owners Be Willing to Pay?" *New Scientist*, August 27, 2005.
Sam Kazman	"The Scapegoat Utility Vehicle," *Ideas on Liberty*, July/August 2003.
David LaGesse	"My Car, the Informer," *U.S. News & World Report*, March 21, 2005.
Alexander Marriott	"Give Me Liberty or Give Me Seatbelt Laws?" *Capitalism Magazine*, December 28, 2003.
Dale P. Murphy and Catherine Maxwell	"Elderly Drivers: When Is It Time to Take the Keys Away?" *Consultant*, January 2005.
Eric Nagourney	"Impaired Driving on the Rise," *New York Times*, April 26, 2005.
John O'Neil	"Double Trouble Behind the Wheel," *New York Times*, September 2, 2003.
Jerry Taylor	"Stop! Don't Ditch Your SUV Just Yet," *National Review Online*, February 4, 2003.

CHAPTER 3

How Should Youth Driving Be Regulated?

Chapter Preface

D riving an automobile can be a risky activity whatever your age—in 2004, 42,636 people lost their lives in automobile crashes in the United States—however, statistics show that when the driver is young, the risk increases. According to the National Highway Traffic Safety Administration (NHTSA), automobile crashes are the leading cause of death for young people aged fifteen to twenty. The Insurance Institute for Highway Safety estimates that motor vehicle crashes account for 40 percent of adolescent fatalities. Drivers between fifteen and twenty years of age make up only 6.4 percent of the nation's driving population, but for the last ten years they have been involved in approximately 14 percent of all fatal car crashes. As these figures show, concern over youth driving and how it should be regulated is well justified.

Experts generally agree that one of the major factors contributing to unsafe youth driving is simple inexperience. Youths are still practicing their driving skills and, in many cases, they lack the knowledge or experience to help them deal with unexpected driving conditions. Virginia driving school owner Larry Blake has experienced this personally. He believes his profession is one of the most dangerous because he is riding with inexperienced teenage drivers who have not yet learned how to deal with some of the road conditions they encounter. "They're always either understeering or oversteering," says Blake, "going off the road or hitting the curb, or turning too soon or too late." Studies conducted by the Insurance Institute for Highway Safety support the belief that youth driving improves through driving experience. The studies show that the accident rate for youth drivers drops by approximately two-thirds after their first seven hundred miles of driving.

Another cause of unsafe youth driving is immaturity. Experts contend that young people often drive impulsively, make poor judgments, and are more likely to take risks on the road. All of these factors increase the chances of them being involved in an accident. For example, according to NHTSA, a larger proportion of crashes killing teens involve speeding or going too fast for road conditions, compared to accidents involving other drivers. Teens are also the least likely age group to wear a seat belt and the most likely to drink and drive, two risk-taking behaviors that significantly increase the chance of harm on the road. According to the Centers for Disease Control and Prevention, 29 percent of teens killed in automobile crashes in 2002 had been drinking, and 77 percent were not wearing seat belts.

Clearly, youth drivers pose a higher-than-average risk to themselves and to everyone else on the road, and most analysts recognize the need for youth driving restrictions. However, there is a lack of consensus over exactly what regulations should be passed to make youth driving safer. The authors of the following viewpoints offer some opinions on this important topic.

> *"Authorities need to get the racers off the streets and onto dragstrips and racetracks. . . . And, sorry, but nobody under 18 should be allowed to participate."*

Authorities Should Stop Teens from Engaging in Street Racing

Denver Post

Street racing has become increasingly popular in Colorado and elsewhere, claims this editorial from the Denver Post. *Despite its popularity, however, the* Post *believes this sport is extremely dangerous to both racers and spectators. In addition, it poses a risk to other citizens who might accidentally encounter a race while driving at night. The editorial urges law enforcement officials to allow racing only at dragstrips and racetracks, and maintains that teenagers under eighteen years old should never be allowed to participate.*

As you read, consider the following questions:

1. How did street racing become popular, as argued by the author?
2. According to the author, what speeds do drag racers often exceed?
3. In the author's opinion, what is the advantage of rac-

The Denver Post, "No Need for Speed," October 23, 2003, p. B6. Copyright © 2003 by *The Denver Post*. Reproduced by permission.

ing at legal dragstrips and racetracks instead of on the streets?

We have Hollywood to thank for popularizing the dangerous sport known as street racing—with special credit to 'The Fast and the Furious,' a nitro-fueled, testosterone-charged action thriller from two summers ago [2002].

Never mind the vapid plot (or, more accurately, non-plot), the movie featuring muscular Vin Diesel as the leader of a gang of motorheads who also hijacked trucks grossed $41 million its first weekend.

Now, the allure of gleaming custom paint jobs, howling turbocharged engines and the piercing scream of rubber on pavement has brought this illegal activity from the silver screen to a Denver street near you.

Last weekend [October 2003], Denver cops launched a major crackdown on street racers, arresting 50 people and confiscating 10 of the high-powered cars. Not only was the fad imported from California, so was the solution. The Los Angeles Police Department, among others, has employed massive sweeps and confiscates cars to curtail street racing.

Dangerous to All

On the coast, some of the illegal contests are drag races, but others run late at night on designated courses on deserted streets in industrial areas. (The Denver variety is drag racing.) Speeds often exceed 140 mph. Locations are posted on Internet sites.

Souped-up vehicles usually are import sedans such as Hondas and Acuras modified (often for tens of thousands of dollars) to squeeze as much horsepower and speed as possible out of the engine. In the movie, at least, the cars also had expensive touches such as machined rims, wide-profile tires and custom paint.

"A Prescription for Death"

Authorities say young drivers are involved in illegal street-racing more often than parents know and more often than available statistics show. Last year [2003], more juveniles went to court on racing charges than in 2000. And high tech equipment has enabled teens and young adults to dramatically boost the speed of their cars. . . .

"When you put together young drivers, no seat belts, souped-up cars and speeds of 90 or 100 miles an hour, it's just a prescription for death," says Ohio Rep. Gary Cates. . . .

While many parents are clueless about engine modifications, others knowingly help their kids add parts to crank up their cars' speeds.

"What's shocked the hell out of me the most is that a lot of these parents know that their kids have this stuff on their cars—and they're OK with it," said Butler County [Ohio] Sheriff's Chief Deputy Richard K. Jones. "It's like saying: 'Here are the keys to this rocket. Go drive this rocket 140 miles an hour—and it's OK.'" . . .

Police Sgt. Barry Walker said young drivers, racing or not, tend to test their cars' capabilities:

"Every car and every driver has a point at which they're going to lose control. They keep pushing the limits until one final time when they push what they or their cars can do—and they run out of luck," he said.

Janice Morse, Cincinnati Enquirer, *July 25, 2004.*

A macho car? Thumbing your nose at authority? All this at warp speed? Just the sort of thing that appeals to youngsters no less immune to aping what they see on the screen than their parents were.

And they also think they're indestructible. But they're not. On Oct. 16, 17-year-old Jimmy Griffin, a junior at Legacy High School, was fatally injured in a two-car crash in Westminster. The boy and two friends were drag racing when their vehicles collided and flipped at about 90 mph. His was only the most recent such fatality in Colorado.

Police say that street racing is dangerous not only to participants but also to spectators who gather to watch the races. Aficionados claim they look for places with no nighttime traffic, but there's always a risk that some innocent citizen working the late shift might get T-boned on the way home.

Stop Street Racing

Metro-area authorities need to get the racers off the streets and onto dragstrips and racetracks where they can compete without endangering others. And, sorry, but nobody under 18 should be allowed to participate.

"Live fast, die young and leave a good-looking corpse" may sound good in old '50s flicks, but in the real world, the death of a young person is a tragedy that robs his family and society of incalculable promise.

"[Supervised racing ensures that] no kid crosses a double yellow line and collides head-on with a vehicle driven by a single father trying to raise three motherless children."

Teens Should Be Encouraged to Participate in Supervised Street Racing

Leonard Sax

In the following viewpoint Leonard Sax argues that many teenagers have a natural desire to engage in street racing because it is so dangerous. He also maintains that education is not an effective way to prevent this dangerous activity. Instead, says Sax, the most effective way to prevent teenagers from participating in street racing is to let them race on designated racetracks, under adult supervision. Sax is a physician and psychologist who practices in Montgomery County, Maryland.

As you read, consider the following questions:

1. How do girls differ from boys in regard to risk taking, according to Sax?

2. Why did a 1997 government campaign to stop teenage drug use fail, as explained by the author?

3. According to Sax, what was the number of fatalities

due to reckless driving and street racing before and after the first year of the RaceLegal program?

I met Danny Sivert seven years ago [1997], I was with him in June 2002 after his wife, Bette, was killed in a traffic accident, leaving him to raise their three young children alone.

On Nov. 19 Danny was driving home when two young men lost control of their pickup on Maryland Route 80, slid across the center line and struck Danny's pickup head-on. A helicopter airlifted Danny to the Shock Trauma Center in Baltimore, but he died later that evening.

An Epidemic of Reckless Driving

We are in an epidemic of death and injury caused by reckless driving. That's not just my assessment. "Epidemic" is the word Stephen Bender, an epidemiologist and professor emeritus in the graduate school of public health at San Diego State University, uses to describe the surging numbers of injuries and deaths nationwide caused by young men driving recklessly.

Robyn Solomon, president of the Winston Churchill High School Parent Teacher Student Association, used the same word after a 16-year-old boy from that school died in a Nov. 13 [2004] car accident. "Parents need to be talking to their kids and explaining to them the risk," Solomon said.

Area police agree. Montgomery County police are targeting teenagers with an education campaign. But we can't stop the epidemic of death and injury caused by reckless driving just by telling teenagers about the risks.

Education May Not Be the Answer

I've worked with teenagers who abuse drugs. In the 1980s, we believed that the best way to discourage illegal drug use was to warn teenagers about the risks, but research in the ensuing two decades uncovered dramatic gender differences in outcomes from that approach. Most girls responded to the fa-

For the Rush

Why do teens insist on street racing? Some say it's the adrenaline rush. "It's indescribable really. It's just like power," says Paul Smith, 18. Paul was sent to jail and had his license suspended for street racing. Justin, 22, agrees: "Adrenaline, you can't beat it. It's the worst drug; you know, you got some, you want more. You got power; you want more. You never stop." . . .

For some kids, speed is exhilarating, and the risk of dying isn't very real.

Emily Halevy, "Illegal Street Racing," www.kget.com, 2005.

mous, "This is your brain. This is your brain on drugs" commercial. But not boys—especially the sensation-seeking, risk-taking ones who are most likely to use illegal drugs.

In 1997 the federal government launched a nationwide advertising program designed to decrease teenage drug use. Five years later, it sheepishly announced that the $900 million campaign had "flopped." Teenagers who saw the government commercials were more likely to use drugs than teenagers who had never seen them. I suspect that was especially true for teenage boys. So more education may not be the answer for the problem of reckless driving either.

Teenage boys who drive down public roads at 90 mph know they are doing something dangerous. They're doing it, in part, because of the danger. Telling them that it's dangerous isn't likely to get them to stop. It might even spur them on. So if more education isn't the answer, what is?

The RaceLegal Program

Bender, the San Diego State professor who called reckless driving an epidemic, has taken a pioneering approach to the problem. In 2002 there were 16 deaths and 31 serious injuries attributed to reckless driving and street racing in San Diego. With funding from the California Office of Traffic Safety, Bender began a program he calls RaceLegal. On Friday evenings, the city's young people—mostly teenage boys and young men—gather at a four-lane, one-eighth-mile-long drag strip in a corner of a San Diego stadium. On a typical Friday, about 300 would-be racers appear. Their cars are checked for safety features, and all drivers must wear helmets. The races, mostly time trials, often go past midnight.

In 2003, the first year that the RaceLegal program was in action, the number of fatalities in San Diego fell to four. So far this year [2004] San Diego has had no deaths attributed to reckless driving or street racing.

Bender's idea is catching on across the country. In Noble, Okla., drivers can pay $15 to race on Friday evenings at the Thunder Valley Raceway Park. "Beat the Heat" events on the second Friday of every month match high school kids racing their own cars against Noble's police officers driving police cruisers. Similar programs have begun in Atlanta, Las Vegas and Muncie, Ind.

One thing's for sure: What we're doing right now isn't working in Montgomery County or in the greater Washington area. "Most public policies [including high school education programs] have had little impact on the problem" of reckless driving, according to a report issued earlier this year by the Insurance Institute for Highway Safety.

Worth a Try

So maybe we should try Bender's idea. . . .

Some people are uncomfortable with the idea of supervised racing. Allowing teenagers with no special training to race at speeds of more than 100 mph obviously involves some risk. However, at RaceLegal venues, no kid crosses a double yellow line and collides head-on with a vehicle driven by a single father trying to raise three motherless children.

I'm all for stricter enforcement of laws against reckless driving. But as Montgomery County Police Chief J. Thomas Manger said after another teenager died in a motor vehicle accident, "The answer is not more cops. We can only do so much."

A college fund has been established for the children of Danny and Bette Sivert, and my wife and I will contribute to it. But I think we also should look for ways to stop the epidemic of death and injury caused by reckless driving.

Bender's idea deserves a chance.

Dr. Sax is the author of *Why Gender Matters: What Parents and Teachers Need to Know About the Emerging Science of Sex Differences* (Doubleday, 2005).

"Society has an obligation to protect motorists from the risky behavior of underage drinkers."

Efforts to Stop Underage Drunk Driving Must Be Increased

Wendy J. Hamilton

Underage drinking is widespread in the United States, asserts Wendy J. Hamilton in the following viewpoint, which has been excerpted from congressional testimony. In her opinion, the large number of underage drinkers has a high human and economic cost. Underage drunk drivers frequently kill or injure themselves and other passengers and drivers on the roads, says Hamilton. In addition, she maintains, underage drunk driving costs America billions of dollars every year. She believes there must be greater efforts to limit youth access to alcohol, and to prevent intoxicated youth from driving. Hamilton is the national president of Mothers Against Drunk Driving, an organization that works to stop drunk driving and prevent underage drinking.

As you read, consider the following questions:

1. According to Hamilton, of the people who die in traffic crashes involving underage drinking drivers, what percentage are people other than the drivers?

Wendy J. Hamilton, testimony before the U.S. Senate Subcommittee on Substance Abuse and Mental Health Services, Committee on Health, Education, Labor, and Pensions, Washington, DC, September 30, 2003.

2. As cited by the author, while youth make up only 7 percent of the driving population, what percent of alcohol-involved fatal crashes do they comprise?

3. What was the result of increasing the minimum drinking age to twenty-one, according to Hamilton?

M y name is Wendy Hamilton and I am the National President of Mothers Against Drunk Driving [MADD]. MADD's mission is to stop drunk driving, support the victims of this violent crime and prevent underage drinking. I am honored to be here today to testify on the critical public health issue of illegal youth alcohol use. . . .

The Problem

Without question, alcohol is the most widely used drug among America's youth. It is illegal for people under the age of 21 to drink alcohol, and yet currently there are 10.1 million underage drinkers in this nation (2002 National Household Survey On Drug Use and Health). Alcohol kills 6.5 times more kids than all other illicit drugs combined and is a major factor in the three leading causes of death of America's teens: motor vehicle crashes, homicides and suicides. Underage drinking does not just harm the drinker: half of the people who die in traffic crashes involving underage drinking drivers are people other than the drinking drivers. Underage drinking is not harmless fun. There is no such thing as "responsible" underage drinking.

Progress was made in the 1980's, most notably with the raising of the minimum drinking age to 21—a law that has saved over 20,000 young lives. But we still have a national mentality that accepts underage drinking as a mere "rite of passage," and underage drinking rates remain inexcusably high and have not improved for the past decade.

According to 2002 Monitoring the Future data, nearly half (48.6 percent) of all high school seniors report drinking in the last 30 days, a much larger proportion of youth than those who report either using marijuana (21.5 percent) or smoking (26.7 percent). The proportion of high school seniors who report drinking in the last 30 days was the same in 2002 as it was in 1993. Additionally, 29 percent of seniors report having five or more drinks on at least one occasion in the past two weeks, a percentage virtually unchanged since 1993. . . .

Drunk Driving

The consequences of youth alcohol use are staggering. Research demonstrates that the younger someone starts drinking, the more likely they are to suffer from alcohol-related problems later in life, including alcohol dependence and drunk driving. Children who drink before age 15 are four times more likely to become alcohol dependent than those who delay drinking until they are 21.

More than 17,000 people are killed each year in alcohol-related crashes and approximately one-half million are injured. In 2000, 69 percent of youth killed in alcohol-related traffic crashes involved underage drinking drivers. Although young drivers make up a mere 7 percent of the driving population, they constitute 13 percent of the alcohol-involved drivers in fatal crashes.

Underage Drinking Data

Underage drinking remains a persistent problem among youth. About 10.7 million Americans between ages 12–20 report current alcohol use; this represents nearly 29% of this age group for whom alcohol is illegal. . . .

• A driver aged 16 or 17 years old is more likely to be fatally injured in a motor vehicle crash as the number of passengers in the vehicle increases, according to a report from Johns Hopkins University.

• According to [a 2003 study], drinking and driving continues to be an issue of great importance to teens. Thirty-five percent of teens cite drinking and driving as one of the top five issues they strongly care about —it ranks second as their most-pressing social concern.

• Young drivers are over represented in both alcohol- and non-alcohol related fatality rates. Alcohol-related fatality rates are nearly twice as great for 18-, 19- and 20-year-olds as for the population over 21. More than 40 percent of 18-, 19-, and 20-year-old crash fatalities are alcohol related.

Century Council, 2005, www.centurycouncil.org.

The 1999 National Survey of Drinking and Driving Among Drivers Age 16–20 revealed that youth drove 11 million times after drinking in the past year. Their average blood alcohol level was .10 percent, three times the level of all drivers who drove after drinking. Forty percent of youth who drove after drinking had a least one passenger in the vehicle. Clearly young drivers are putting themselves at risk, but they are also putting others at risk. Society has an obligation to protect motorists from the risky behavior of underage drinkers. Society also has an obligation to protect kids from themselves. . . .

In addition to the human costs associated with underage drinking, the economic cost to society is staggering. It is conservatively estimated that underage drinking costs this nation $53 billion dollars each year, including $19 billion from traffic crashes and $29 billion from violent crime. The NAS [National Academy of Science] points out that this estimate is "somewhat incomplete" and "does not include medical costs other than those associated with traffic crashes" and other potential factors contributing to the social costs of underage drinking. The NAS concludes that "the $53 billion appears to be an underestimate of the social costs of underage drinking."
. . .

Efforts to Combat Underage Drinking Are Inadequate

While illicit drugs and tobacco youth prevention have received considerable attention and funding from the federal government, underage drinking has consistently been ignored. NAS confirms this:

> In fiscal 2000, the nation spent approximately $1.8 billion on preventing illicit drug use (Office of National Drug Control Policy, 2003), which was 25 times the amount, $71.1 million, targeted at preventing underage alcohol use.

Not only is there minimal funding available to states and local communities specifically targeted to reduce youth alcohol use, there is also no coordinated national effort to reduce and prevent underage drinking.

In May 2001 the General Accounting Office (GAO) released a report outlining federal funds aimed at preventing underage drinking. The report provided concrete evidence that: 1) the federal government's approach to youth alcohol use prevention is disjointed and 2) funding for youth alcohol prevention is woefully inadequate.

GAO found that multiple federal agencies play some role in underage drinking prevention, and that only a very small portion—7 percent—of total funds available for alcohol and other drug use both had a specific focus on alcohol and identified youth or youth and the broader community as the specific target population. Specifically, among the Departments of Health and Human Services, Justice and Transportation, a mere $71.1 million dollars focused on youth or alcohol and youth and the broader community. . . .

Limiting Alcohol Access to Youth

Limiting youth access to alcohol is a proven way to decrease underage drinking. Most notably, increasing the minimum drinking age to 21 has been one of the most effective public health policies in history, resulting in a significant decrease in fatal traffic crashes, DWI [driving while intoxicated] arrests, and self-reported drinking by young people. However, the law alone does not preclude youth from gaining access to alcohol. General deterrence through sanctions, improved enforcement, and public awareness of enforcement is needed in order to effectively implement restrictions on youth alcohol use.

The NAS report points out that "it is apparently not difficult for youth who want to drink to readily obtain alcohol. A majority of high school students, even eighth graders, report that alcohol is 'fairly easy' or 'very easy' to get, with the proportion increasing from eighth to tenth to twelfth grade." For eighth graders, 60 percent report that alcohol is fairly easy or very easy to obtain, while for twelfth graders the percentage is more than 90 percent. The NAS also reports that the "alcohol most favored by underage drinkers is beer."

A critical component of a comprehensive strategy to reduce underage drinking is to enact and strengthen laws designed to limit youth alcohol consumption. Although every state defines the legal minimum drinking age at 21, state laws vary in scope in terms of restrictions relating to underage purchase, possession, or consumption of alcohol and for the use of false identification. These weaknesses, as NAS points out, compromise the effectiveness of minimum drinking age laws.

The NAS recommendations to limit youth alcohol use focus on enacting and strengthening laws to: 1) reduce access through commercial sources; 2) reduce access through non-commercial sources; 3) reduce drinking and driving by underage drinkers; and 4) prescribe and enforce penalties on adult providers and underage drinkers.

In addition to closing loopholes in age 21 laws as mentioned above, NAS suggests, and MADD agrees, implementing key approaches to meeting these goals, including:

- Imposing more stringent penalties on retail licensees for violation of laws against sales to minors;

- Strengthening compliance check programs in retail outlets; . . .

- Regulating internet sales and home delivery of alcohol;

- Holding adults responsible for illegal consumption of alcohol by minors;

- Implementing beer keg registration laws to deter the purchase of kegs of beer for consumption by minors;

- Strengthening enforcement of zero tolerance laws;

- Implementing the use of routine sobriety checkpoints to increase the deterrence of underage drinking and driving. . . .

Time to Take Action

It is time for our nation—from parents to communities to our political leaders at the national and state levels—to end the complacent attitude about underage drinking and to take action to end this public health epidemic. There is an urgent need to expand prevention, treatment and community programs and improve enforcement of existing laws to prevent underage drinking. More youth drink alcohol than smoke tobacco or use other illegal drugs, yet federal investments in preventing underage drinking pale in comparison with resources targeted at preventing illicit drug use.

The media constantly reports on the countless numbers of alcohol-related deaths and injuries of today's youth, but our nation accepts and even enables these preventable tragedies. The future of our nation's youth continues to hang in the balance. Underage drinking is illegal, and yet millions of kids continue to engage in this high-risk behavior every month, every weekend, and even every day. . . .

The devastating effects of underage drinking are completely preventable. . . . We must, as a nation, ramp up our efforts, and today is a new beginning in that endeavor.

| "*Teen drinking and teen drunk-driving fatalities have declined significantly over the last two decades.*"

Underage Drunk Driving Has Decreased

Francine Katz

The following viewpoint is excerpted from congressional testimony by Francine Katz, vice president of corporate communications for brewing company Anheuser-Busch. According to Katz, Anheuser-Busch engages in numerous programs aimed at preventing underage drinking and drunk driving. These efforts include education for teenagers, parents, and alcohol retailers, she says. In Katz's opinion, as a result of actions by Anheuser-Busch, teenage drunk driving has declined significantly in the United States. This progress is particularly significant, she says, considering that the number of licensed teenage drivers has actually increased.

As you read, consider the following questions:

1. How does Anheuser-Busch help parents fight underage drinking, as explained by the author?
2. Why do alcohol retailers play a significant role in preventing underage drinking, as explained by Katz?
3. According to the Department of Transportation, as cited by the author, by what percentage did teenage

Francine Katz, testimony before the U.S. House Subcommittee on Education Reform, Committee on Education, Washington, DC, February 11, 2004.

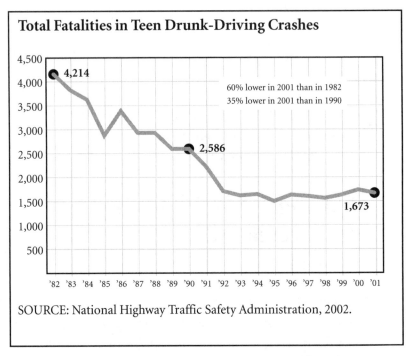

Total Fatalities in Teen Drunk-Driving Crashes

4,214

60% lower in 2001 than in 1982
35% lower in 2001 than in 1990

2,586

1,673

SOURCE: National Highway Traffic Safety Administration, 2002.

drunk driving crashes decrease between 1982 and 2002?

M y name is Francine Katz, and I'm the vice president responsible for [brewing company] Anheuser-Busch's long-standing efforts to fight alcohol abuse, an area I have been working in since 1990. I also am the mother of a 17-year-old daughter and a 12-year-old son, so I am dealing with these issues as a parent, too. . . .

Preventing Underage Drinking

Those of us in the beer industry are also in the hospitality business. Our beers are intended to be a refreshing accompaniment to social occasions or a simple reward after a long day's work. We take great pride in being part of an industry that has had its roots in America since colonial times. We also understand the responsibility that goes along with making and marketing an adult product, and we have been at the forefront of efforts to fight the abuse of our products. I am proud to tell you that my company has invested nearly a half billion dollars thus far in these efforts, and we are committed to continuing these initiatives. And I speak for other members of our nation's beer industry. While we compete with each other as fiercely as any industry in America, in this we are united: we don't want kids to drink, and we are committed to giving parents and others who deal with the problem real solutions. . . .

We all agree that underage drinking is a serious issue that we must aggressively fight. And I hope that we can channel our energies and resources toward this collective goal and find ways to work together in this fight.

A Three-Prong Approach

We believe the most effective way to fight underage drinking is to use a three-prong approach, and the cornerstone of that approach is focused on parents. . . .

Accordingly, we have invested a significant amount of our efforts in programs for parents. One such program, a guide book and video for parents called "Family Talk About Drinking," was created by an advisory panel of authorities from the areas of family counseling, alcohol treatment and education. It is available in five languages. We promote this free program through advertising and on our website, but over the years, we have also worked in partnership with groups and organizations across the country to get these materials into the hands of parents. . . .

The second prong to our efforts to fight underage drinking is aimed at the retail level, the point-of-purchase. Under the laws governing the sale and distribution of beer, we do not sell our products to consumers. Rather, we sell to our wholesalers, they sell to retailers and retailers sell to the public. As a result, retailers are on the front lines and they play a vital role in stopping underage drinking. In cooperation with police departments, county sheriffs, and other state and local agencies, we have worked aggressively to help retailers and servers stop sales to minors. We provide materials in English, Spanish, Korean and Vietnamese for retailers to teach them how to properly check IDs and to spot fake IDs. We also disseminate "WE ID" and other point-of-sale materials that remind customers that the establishment will ask for proper identification. Among the myriad of tools we provide retailers are such things as drivers license booklets that show valid licenses from all 50 states and serve as a useful tool for retailers—especially in college communities—who are confronted with IDs from all over the country. We have worked closely in these efforts with a number of major national retailers including 7-Eleven Stores, Circle K, Publix and Safeway Markets to put these materials to work in their stores. Our efforts in this regard were just featured in one of our Super Bowl commercials earlier this month [February 2004], in which an attentive clerk deterred two teens in their attempt to buy beer. . . .

Finally, the third prong of our approach involves directing efforts at young people, to help them make good decisions. The most visible example of these efforts is a Speakers Bureau comprised of third parties from many walks of life who take their messages directly into schools. The members of the Anheuser-Busch Consumer Awareness and Education Speakers Bureau bring a message of responsibility and respect for the law to middle school and high school students around the country. With the support of our local wholesalers, over the past five years, these speakers have reached more than 1.4 million students via 4,700 presentations throughout the country. . . .

Significant Progress

[It is] important to cite the progress that has been made on this front—to let parents know their efforts are working, and to salute those teens who are making the right decisions. And many are. Teen drinking and teen drunk-driving fatalities have declined significantly over the last two decades. According to the U.S. Department of Health and Human Services, 82% of today's adolescents do not drink. That means nearly 20 million adolescents are doing the right thing by *not* drinking. Similarly, according to the University of Michigan survey called "Monitoring the Future," sponsored by the National Institute on Drug Abuse, the percentage of high school seniors who report having a drink in the last 30 days was 32% lower in 2002 than it was in 1982. In 2003, there were nearly 410,000 fewer high school seniors who reported past-month drinking than did in 1982. And beer consumption by college freshmen fell 39% in the same time frame according to the American Council on Education and researchers at the University of California at Los Angeles. The latter two measurements are record lows.

In addition, the United States Department of Transportation reports that fatalities in crashes involving drunk drivers aged 16 to 20 have fallen 61% between 1982 and 2002. There were 2,500 fewer teen drunk-driving fatalities in 2002 than there were in 1982. That progress has been achieved even though the number of 16 to 20-year-olds licensed to drive has increased over 7% over the last decade to more than 12.4 million.

"*Graduated driver's license (GDL) laws ... decrease accident rates for teen drivers.*"

Driving Restrictions Decrease Youth Accident Rates

Melissa Savage

In the following viewpoint Melissa Savage argues in favor of graduated driver's license laws and other restrictions on teenage drivers. Inexperience and immaturity mean that young drivers are more likely to crash than adults, maintains Savage. She believes the best solution to this problem is to restrict teen driving to daylight hours and to forbid teens under eighteen years old from driving with other teens. This approach has been proven to reduce teen accident rates, she says. Savage is a contributing writer to State Legislatures.

As you read, consider the following questions:

1. In 2001, what was the cost to taxpayers from car wrecks involving teenage drivers, as cited by the author?

2. According to Savage, what happened to fatality and injury rates among teenagers in Florida after a graduated driver's license law was adopted?

Melissa Savage, "Surviving Driving: Immaturity and Inexperience Add Up to Disaster for Many Teen Drivers. Some 6,000 Are Killed Each Year and 300,000 Injured. But State Laws Can Reduce the Risks," *State Legislatures*, vol. 30, February 2004, p. 16.

3. According to the Insurance Institute for Highway Safety, as cited by the author, by how much does just one teen passenger in a car increase the crash risk?

For teens, the license to drive is the key to freedom. The end of humiliating trips in the family van with mom or dad at the wheel. The end of waiting for a ride. The big step toward adulthood.

For parents, it's another kind of freedom. The end of carpooling and chauffeuring headaches. But it also is sleepless nights waiting for a young driver to come home.

Each year 6,000 don't, and their parents live their worst nightmare: receiving the dreaded phone call telling them that their child has been killed in a crash. For 300,000 more parents each year, it means learning that their young driver has been injured.

Teens are more likely to speed and tailgate and less likely to wear seat belts than older drivers. It's no wonder accident rates for this age group are high. The National Safety Council reports that 20 percent of 16-year-old drivers will be involved in a crash at some point during their first year of driving—the accident rate is the highest during the first month. And 16-year-old drivers are three times more likely to end up in a wreck than older teens.

The big step toward adulthood comes with tremendous responsibility—and the need to make mature choices.

But teens are often ill-equipped to make the split-second decisions that can keep them safe on the road. Inexperience and immaturity behind the wheel is the leading cause of death for teens.

Crashes not only cause serious physical and emotional pain, they are costly. In 2001, car wrecks involving teen drivers cost taxpayers $42.3 billion for emergency services, medical and rehabilitation costs, productivity losses and property damage, according to the National Highway Traffic Safety Administration.

Once teens gain experience, they are safer and less likely to crash, studies show.

Times Have Changed

Until the mid-1990s, all it took for most teens to get their license was reaching their 16th birthday, a written exam and a road test. Teens were free to drive anywhere, any time with anyone. But times have changed. Now graduated driver's license laws appear to be saving young lives.

The Insurance Institute for Highway Safety recommends that states implement a learner's phase that begins at age 16, lasts at least six months and includes 30 to 50 hours of supervised driving. The group recommends an intermediate phase that lasts until age 18 and includes a restriction on driving after 9 or 10 P.M. and no teen passengers in the car. Full licensure would be granted at 18.

Graduated driver's license (GDL) laws—even those that may be considered inadequate—do decrease accident rates for teen drivers. In Florida, fatality and injury accidents among 15- to 17-year-old drivers dropped after the law was adopted.

California saw a 23 percent decline in fatal and at-fault injury accidents for 16-year-olds. Teen passenger deaths decreased by 40 percent after its GDL law went into effect.

Curbing Teen Deaths

Traffic safety experts believe that restricting teen nighttime driving during the critical hours of 9 to 11 P.M. and limiting the number of teen passengers to only one, or ideally to none, are the best ways to curb deaths.

Reduced visibility, glare from oncoming traffic and fatigue make nighttime a challenge for all drivers, but especially for teens. The risk of being killed at night is especially high for beginning drivers—nearly three times higher than during the

Asay. © 1996 by Creators Syndicate, Inc. Reproduced by permission.

day for 16-year-olds—according to a study in the *Journal of Safety Research*. Restrictions that allow teens to drive at night with supervision lower the number of crashes during restricted hours by as much as 60 percent, the journal says.

North Carolina teens must be off the roads from 9 P.M. to 5 A.M. Idaho restricts teen drivers from sunset to sunrise. In South Carolina, teen drivers aren't allowed on the roads from 6 P.M. to 6 A.M.

Nighttime driving restrictions are not meant to be curfews, but rather to encourage supervised driving. "Most states already have curfews in place so teens shouldn't be out anyway," says Ashley Connors, Students Against Destructive Decisions student of the year.

She also believes that these laws encourage teens to make better choices, which can be hard when faced with peer pressure. "If a law is in place, it's easier to say no to risky behavior. The law backs them up," she says.

Limiting Distractions

Maine and New Jersey recognize that young drivers talking on their cell phones are not focused on the road, so they have outlawed it for drivers under age 21.

Traffic safety advocates expect more states to pass similar laws in the future since studies have shown that new drivers are not able to drive safely and talk on the phone simultaneously.

Teen passengers pose another risk. Just one other teen in the car increases the crash risk by 50 percent, according to the Insurance Institute for Highway Safety. Three or more passengers increase the risk of a wreck by four times more than if the teen is driving alone.

California bans teens transporting anyone under the age of 20 for the first six months of their provisional licenses, unless accompanied by a parent or adult over 25. Teens can drive without supervision if the young passengers are family members, and a parent approves.

A 2003 Illinois law prohibits teens under 18 from driving with more than one passenger under age 20. Exceptions to the law include siblings and other family members. "This is a great bill," says Senator John Cullerton who sponsored it. "There was no organized opposition to it. And once suburban moms heard the statistics, they were supportive."

Although the Illinois bill faced little opposition, one in Maryland did. Sponsored by Delegate Adrienne Mandel, the bill would have prohibited drivers under 18 from transporting any teen passengers during the first six months of their provisional licenses. After that, they could drive with only one teen passenger until they turned 18. The bill was designed to restrict the "usual rolling party of seven, eight, nine teens crammed into a vehicle, and it's easy for police to enforce," says Mandel.

Opponents argued that restricting passengers would result

in more teen drivers on the road. Others wanted exemptions for teenage family members to ride as passengers.

Delegate Mandel will introduce the bill again this session because "no GDL law is complete without a passenger restriction."[1]

Traffic experts support the kinds of restrictions in graduated driver's license bills. "Our objective is not to write more tickets, prohibit teens from driving or get in the way of family mobility," says Chuck Hurley, vice president of the National Safety Council. "We know how we can reduce crashes, injuries and fatalities. We know how we can save families and society money. We know how we can spare families, high schools and communities painful and numbing tragedies. And we should do that."

1. This bill did not pass.

> *"Every driver ... should be required to take a classroom and behind-the-wheel course from a professional driving instructor."*

Better Driver Education Will Make Young Drivers Safer

Reno Gazette-Journal

Driving is a difficult activity that requires complex skills, maintains this editorial from the Reno Gazette-Journal. *The editors believe that teenage drivers are not receiving sufficient education to help them develop these skills and are thus involved in an increasing number of car crashes. In addition, argues the authors, most adults do not set a good driving example for youth. According to the* Gazette-Journal, *teenagers should have their driving restricted and receive comprehensive driving education from professional driving instructors. The* Reno Gazette-Journal *is a daily online and print newspaper serving the Reno, Nevada, area.*

As you read, consider the following questions:

1. Why are parents not the best teachers for young drivers, according to the author?

2. As cited by the author, of the 187 people killed in Nevada accidents involving teen drivers from 1999 to 2003, how many were passengers?

3. In the author's opinion, what should be required of teens before they receive a permanent license at age 18?

I f we want our teenagers to take driving seriously, we have to take driving seriously.

That we're not doing that now is obvious on the streets and highways of Northern Nevada every day. We speed, we ignore signs, we don't bother with turn signals, we step on it as we run yellow lights, we step on it as we run red lights, we drive while drinking hot coffee or talking animatedly on the phone, we do things that would scare us to death if we saw our kids doing the same thing.

How can we expect anything better than that from the teenagers who have been watching us drive for all of their lives?

We can't!

A Difficult Skill

Driving is a complex set of skills that requires study, manual dexterity, good eyesight, judgment, concentration and maturity. Yet we treat it as one more rite of passage, like downing a few beers on your 21st birthday. We say it's the parents' responsibility to teach a youngster all of the skills they need to drive and to make smart decisions while handling thousands of pounds of automobile on a busy street. So we let amateurs distracted by the many responsibilities of parenthood handle a youngster's education—amateurs who themselves were taught by amateurs and prove every day that they weren't paying attention to all of their lessons.

Is it any wonder that teens are getting into more accidents every year (an increase of 20 percent between 1999 and 2002 in Washoe County [Nevada], according to an RGJ [*Reno Gazette-Journal*] analysis published in the special section

Developing Skills

Driver education can help provide the foundation for safe behaviors through knowledge and practicing beginning skills. Driver education should be viewed as the beginning of a process through which teens learn valuable driving skills and the experience necessary to make them safe drivers. Parents should not rely solely on driver education to provide teens the significant knowledge and experience that they need to become safe drivers. Too often, completing driver education is viewed as the end of the learning process, rather than the beginning. In some states, the completion of driver education qualifies a teen for full driving privileges. The National Safety Council believes this is not a wise approach. Research has shown that significant hours of behind-the-wheel experience are necessary to reduce crash involvement risk.

National Safety Council, June 22, 2005, www.nsc.org.

"Collision Course: The case for tougher restrictions on Nevada's teenage drivers" on Sept. 25 [2005]). The number of injury accidents also increased (by 30 percent), as did the number of fatal accidents involving teen drivers statewide (up 60 percent).

If it were just the drivers who were being hurt by the lack of good driving skills, perhaps we could argue that it's the parents' responsibility. But it's not. They're also killing their friends and siblings (more than half of the 187 people killed in accidents involving teen drivers from 1999–2003 were passengers). It's not just someone else's kid; it's ours, too.

Better Driver Education

What can we do about it?

First, we have to stop telling teenagers that driving is just a matter of keeping the car between the lines. Speeding isn't wrong only when you get caught. And the rules of the road aren't just for the other guy.

Then we have to get serious about the requirements for getting a driver's license . . . and follow up.

The new rules that went into effect Saturday [October 1, 2005] are a good, common sense beginning that unfortunately took several sessions to get through Nevada's Legislature. The minimum age was returned to 16 after being quietly reduced to 15¾ during a recent special session. Teens younger than 18 will have to hold a learner's permit for six months and demonstrate (with a written log) that they've had 50 hours of behind-the-wheel experience with an adult, including 10 in darkness. They can't transport other teens under 18 for 90 days. And they can't drive between 10 P.M. and 5 A.M. unless going to or coming from school activities or work.

That's along with the long-required classroom work (often completed on the Internet today), and written and driving tests. But it's still not enough.

Every driver, regardless of age, should be required to take a classroom and behind-the-wheel course from a professional driving instructor. Teens should be restricted from transporting passengers for six months, as proposed by State Sen. Barbara Cegavske, R-Las Vegas, for the 2007 Legislature, with food and drink banned, and cell phones turned off. Then they should be required to pass a second set of tests at age 18 to receive a permanent license. And any moving violation should automatically extend the probationary period.

Saving Lives

Teens undoubtedly will see these rules as punitive. They're not. Instead they will ensure that youngsters have the chance to develop all of the skills needed to drive safely and the experience to make good decisions. With luck, they'll live for a long time, bringing that skill and maturity with them.

Best of all, they'd be showing the rest of us how it's supposed to be done. In a generation or two, the idiots we see on the roads today might all be gone and there'd be nothing but well-trained drivers out there. Wouldn't that be great?

Periodical Bibliography

The following articles have been selected to supplement the diverse views presented in this chapter.

Jane Gordon	"Driving Laws Get Tougher for Teenagers, but Is It Enough?" *New York Times*, June 22, 2003.
Kate Kelly	"Wreckless Teens," *U.S. News & World Report*, April 8, 2002.
Fredrick Kunkle	"Safety Experts Doubt Benefits of Driver's Ed; Lots of Practice with Parent Seen as Surest Way to Learn," *Washington Post*, November 22, 2004.
Patrick J. Lowery Jr.	"Curb Illegal Street Racing," *Police Chief*, September 2003.
New York Times	"Teenagers, Cars, and Alcohol," January 23, 2005.
Patrick M. O'Malley and Lloyd D. Johnston	"Unsafe Driving by High School Seniors," *Journal of Studies on Alcohol*, May 2003.
David Ropeik and George Gray	"Cell Phones and Driving: How Risky?" *Consumers' Research Magazine*, January 2003.
Kate Templin	"Teen Drivers and Alcohol: A Deadly Mixture," *CQ Researcher*, January 7, 2005.
William Triplett	"Teen Driving: Should States Impose Tougher Restrictions?" *CQ Researcher*, January 7, 2005.
Patrick Welsh	"Sweet 16: Not for Driving," *USA Today*, November 29, 2004.
Jeanne Wright	"Black Boxes Can Monitor Teen Drivers," *Los Angeles Times*, January 29, 2003.

OPPOSING VIEWPOINTS® SERIES

CHAPTER 4

How Can the United States Meet Its Future Transportation Needs?

Chapter Preface

The United States relies heavily on imported oil to fuel its automobiles and other forms of transportation. According to the U.S. Energy Information Administration, the country imports approximately 12 million barrels of oil every day, with approximately two-thirds of that used for transportation. This amount has been steadily increasing in recent years, and is expected to continue to do so. Thus, any discussion about how America will meet its future transportation needs necessarily includes a debate over where the nation should get its oil. One possible answer, which has been discussed repeatedly over the past twenty-five years, is that the United States should drill for oil in Alaska's Arctic National Wildlife Refuge (ANWR).

ANWR is a 19-million-acre reserve located in northern Alaska. The refuge, created by the U.S. government in 1960, supports a variety of plant and animal life, and encompasses the traditional homelands and subsistence areas of the Inupiaq and Athabascan peoples. Many experts believe that the reserve also contains a vast supply of oil. Immediately to the west of ANWR is Prudhoe Bay, the largest pool of oil ever found in the United States. It is widely believed that ANWR has similar potential. When the reserve was created, oil exploration and drilling there were prohibited, but the prohibition was not irrevocable. Future decisions about oil exploration are to be made by Congress. As of this writing, there have been numerous attempts to allow such exploration, but none have been approved by Congress.

Many groups are in favor of drilling in the area. According to Arctic Power, an organization working to expedite oil exploration in ANWR, "Studies of the ANWR coastal plain indicate it may contain between 6 and 16 billion barrels of recoverable oil." According to the group, "ANWR oil could provide an additional 30 to 50 years of reliable supply." Drilling advocates maintain that it is absurd to ignore such a potentially significant supply, especially considering that the United States imports so much of its oil. Such advocates argue that oil development can be pursued without destroying the area's wildlife. They point to oil development in similar regions to support this contention. According to Arctic Power, "Petroleum development at Prudhoe Bay has not negatively affected wildlife."

In contrast, environmentalists contend that oil development in the refuge will destroy the fragile environment there. According to the Sierra Club, "Drilling in the Arctic National Wildlife Refuge would not put a dent in our dependence on foreign oil, would do nothing to strengthen our national security, and would not save consumers a dime at the pump." The National Resources Defense Council (NRDC) rejects the argument that development will not be harmful to wildlife. The reality is quite the opposite, says NRDC:

> For a sense of what big oil's heavy machinery would do to the refuge, just look . . . [at] Prudhoe Bay—a gargantuan oil complex that has turned 1,000 square miles of fragile tundra into a sprawling industrial zone. . . . The result is a landscape defaced by mountains of sewage sludge, scrap metal, garbage and more than 60 contaminated waste sites.

In 2005 the U.S. Congress once again debated this issue. As of this writing, however, ANWR had not been opened to oil exploration. The debate over oil and ANWR is only one of many fierce disputes related to America's dependence on automobiles for transportation. The authors in the following chapter explore the question of how America will continue to meet its transportation needs in the future.

> "To relieve congestion, our emphasis . . .
> must shift toward dramatic expansion
> of high-capacity public transportation
> systems."

Public Transportation Can Reduce Traffic Congestion

American Public Transportation Association

In the following viewpoint the American Public Transportation Association (APTA) claims that traffic congestion is a serious problem in the United States. According to APTA, congestion has enormous costs in terms of lost hours and wasted fuel, and it causes significant public frustration. The solution to this problem, in the opinion of the organization, is for the United States to invest in expanding its public transportation systems in order to reduce the number of cars on the roads. APTA is a national organization dedicated to strengthening and improving public transportation in the United States.

As you read, consider the following questions:

1. According to the author, how many hours per year does the average person traveling in peak traffic periods waste in congestion delays?

2. While the U.S. population increased by 24 percent between 1980 and 2002, by how much did the num-

ber of registered motor vehicles increase, according to the APTA?

3. As argued by the author, how many cars are removed from the road by a full bus?

A s more and more vehicles crowd the nation's roadways, traffic congestion has an increasingly debilitating effect on our quality of life. Across America, people, business and industry, the economy and the environment pay a higher and higher price for mounting congestion—through delays, lost opportunities, higher costs, increased accidents, reduced competitiveness, pollution, frustration and much more.

The data are clear: Providing fast, affordable, reliable public transportation is essential in blunting the effects of crippling congestion, and providing sustained relief that:

- Protects personal freedom, choice and mobility

- Enhances access to opportunity

- Enables economic prosperity

- Protects our communities and the natural environment

Congestion: A Mounting Problem

The longest-running study of traffic congestion in America—the Urban Mobility Study conducted annually for 19 years by the Texas Transportation Institute (TTI)—confirms the trend: on a daily basis, Americans are experiencing longer delays, longer periods of congestion, and the spread of congestion across more and more of the nation's roadways. This study of 75 urban areas, ranging in size from New York City to areas with 100,000+ population, suggests that traffic congestion will continue to worsen as the number of vehicle miles traveled continues to grow. The data include the following:

- Each person travelling in peak periods wastes, on average, 62 hours a year—nearly eight full working days—in congestion delays.

- Urban travelers can now expect to encounter congested roadways during seven hours of the day.

- Congestion is becoming more widespread, experienced by nearly 60 percent of urban roadways in 2000.

- Congestion is no longer confined to our largest metropolitan areas. As long ago as 1997, two-thirds of peak-period traffic was congested in areas of 500,000 or less.

The Cause

Regardless of whether congestion is recurring (traffic regularly exceeds roadway capacity) or non-recurring (predictable and unpredictable events cause delays), there is one root cause of congestion: too many vehicles crowding available road space coupled with a lack of travel options.

Disproportionate increases in private vehicle use. Population and economic growth spur travel demand, which, in the absence of other travel options, results in disproportionate increases in the use of motor vehicles. From 1980 to 2000, the U.S. population grew 24 percent, while the number of registered motor vehicles increased 46 percent and the number of vehicle miles traveled grew 80 percent.

Chronic under-investment in public transportation and lack of travel alternatives reinforce private vehicle use. Despite recent expansion in public transportation services and resulting record ridership increases in some urban areas, relatively few Americans have access to reasonable or attractive transit options.

- Only 4.3 percent of miles on our road system are served by public transportation.

- Only 49 percent of Americans live within one-quarter mile of a transit stop.

- Nearly 60 percent of the U.S. population lives in major

metropolitan areas of over 1 million, but only 8.3 percent of households have access to subway service.

Business strategies require more road space. "Just-in-time" business strategies designed to keep America competitive in the global economy require smaller but more frequent deliveries, resulting in more freight traffic on our roadways and more congestion.

Public policies reinforce auto-oriented patterns of development. Sprawling development patterns in America's urban and suburban areas often provide no choice but to use private vehicles for every travel need, continually increasing congestion and requiring ever more land devoted to roads and parking.

The Consequences

The breakdown of our street and highway network is exacting a fearsome price across urban and suburban America. The consequences include:

Staggering costs in lost hours, wasted fuel. According to the TTI study, in 2000 the total cost of congestion in terms of lost hours and wasted fuel was $68 billion. Nationwide, the total annual cost may approach $100 billion.

Costs to individuals and families. The personal costs of congestion are also enormous.

- In 2000, each peak-period road user lost $1,160 in wasted fuel and time, including time shared with family and friends. In Las Vegas, for example, where vehicle travel has increased over 80 percent, each motorist pays hundreds of dollars per year in a "hidden tax" due to delays and wasted fuel caused by traffic congestion.

- The cost of owning and operating a vehicle can run as high as $6,000 or more a year. In New York, where public transportation is widely available, 15.3 percent of consumer expenditures go for transportation; in Houston, where there are fewer transportation options, the figure is 23 percent—50 percent higher.

Conserving Energy

Given its high energy efficiency and low polluting, public transportation offers the single largest untapped source of energy savings and environmental gains available to the United States. Throughout much of Europe, people use public transportation for about 10 percent of their daily travel needs. There, governments have long used tax, planning, and regulatory policies to encourage the use of public transportation and protect their urban centers from automobile congestion. Virtually all European governments have also long provided extensive capital and operating assistance to their bus and rail systems. We will see that if Americans used public transportation at the same rate as Europeans—if a little more than ten percent of those who currently use private automobiles shifted to public transportation, or everyone used public transit for about ten percent of their daily travel needs—the United States could be virtually energy independent from Saudi Arabia. The energy savings at that level of public-transit use would be equal to one-quarter of all energy use in the commercial sector in 2000.

Robert J. Shapiro, Kevin A. Hassett, and Frank S. Arnold, American Public Transportation Association, July 2002.

Higher business costs. In an increasingly competitive global economy that relies on "just-in-time" flows of raw materials and finished products, on-time deliveries are critical. Because trucks are the sole providers of goods to 75 percent of American communities, congestion delays increase business costs. As a consequence of the auto dependence that has created our congestion problem, in 2000, $71.5 billion was lost in wages and productivity due to motor vehicle injuries.

Continued dependence on foreign oil. Nearly 43 percent of America's energy resources are used for transportation—compared to industrial use (39 percent) and residential use (11 percent)—and a substantial amount is consumed because of congestion. The 5.7 billion gallons of gasoline wasted in congestion in 2000 (an average of 100 gallons annually by each peak-period road user) would fill 114 supertankers or 570,000 gasoline trucks.

Growing Public Frustration

Traffic congestion is now a top concern of residents across the country. According to the Federal Highway Administration (FHWA), since 1995 traffic flow has been the only roadway characteristic out of eight that has experienced a decline in public satisfaction levels.

The sentiment is expressed in areas around the country. For example, according to 2000 and 2001 surveys in Houston, congestion has become the number one issue, more important than the economy and crime, which topped the charts in previous surveys. In Atlanta, 63 percent of residents favored expanding transportation options or reducing sprawl, compared to 22 percent who favored expanding roads. Across the country, the FHWA found that 7 of 10 respondents favored expanding existing public transportation, while fewer than 4 in 10 favored building more highways to ease traffic problems.

The Solution: Added Emphasis on Public Transportation

Our options are clear. To relieve congestion, our emphasis—and investment priority—must shift toward dramatic expansion of high-capacity public transportation systems, including light rail, heavy rail, commuter rail, bus rapid transit (BRT), express bus services and transit/HOV lanes. This must be coupled with targeted investments in and better management of the current highway network.

The rationales for greater emphasis on transit are powerful.

Public transportation reduces the number of vehicles on the road and vehicle miles traveled. The Maryland Department of Transportation estimates that:

- A full rail car removes 200 cars from the road.
- A full bus removes 60 cars.
- A full van removes 12 cars.

Public transportation reduces hours of delay in major travel corridors. Increased public transportation use reduces delays for both public transportation riders and highway users. According to an FTA [Federal Transit Administration] study of six urban corridors served by high-capacity rail transit:

- Public transportation passengers saved 17,400 hours daily over auto travel in the corridors.
- Remaining road users in the corridors saved 22,000 hours of delay per day due to the absence of vehicles from public transportation users.
- Travelers on surrounding roads in the corridors saved an additional 20,700 hours daily as spillover congestion was reduced.

These reductions represent a savings of $225 million annually in the six corridors analyzed.

Public transportation generates substantial savings to the economy. The FTA values the aggregate benefits from transit-related congestion relief at $19.4 billion annually. Another study indicates that every dollar of public funds invested in public transportation returns up to $6 in economic benefits in urban regions.

Public transportation reduces the need for highway expansion. Highway expansion has become increasingly difficult and controversial. There often is not space, money and public support to add roadway capacity needed to create and sustain acceptable conditions. In addition, there is mounting evidence that additions to highway capacity "induce" added traffic. Increasing lane-miles by one percent may induce a nearly equivalent increase in vehicle-miles of travel within a period as short as five years. By inducing significant traffic, additional road building may do little to reduce congestion.

Benefits Support Other National and Local Goals

Public transportation offers a host of important ancillary benefits by taking the place of private vehicles when and where the highway network is most burdened.

Improved air quality. For every passenger-mile traveled, public transportation produces 95 percent less carbon monoxide, more than 92 percent fewer volatile organic compounds and nearly half as much carbon dioxide and nitrogen oxides.

Reduced energy consumption and dependence. According to [a 2002 study]:

- Energy consumed in transportation in 2000 exceeded the energy consumed in producing all the country's goods.

- Public transportation uses about one-half the fuel of private automobiles, SUVs and light trucks per passenger-mile traveled.

- Public transportation users today save the U.S. the equivalent of one month's oil imports from Saudi Arabia, over 850 million gallons a year or 45 million barrels of oil.

Preservation of land for smarter growth and more productive development. As much as one third of a city's land is devoted to serving the motor vehicles when roads, service stations and parking lots are considered. Public transportation drastically reduces the amount of land needed for cars.

- Urban rail systems can provide more capacity in a 100-foot right-of-way than a six-lane freeway requiring a 300-foot right-of-way.

- Required parking spaces can be reduced 30 and 50 percent, respectively, for office and retail development in transit-intensive areas.

- For a peak-period transit trip, the roadway space and time required for an auto passenger may be 25 times greater than for the time and space required for a bus passenger and 60 times greater than the time and space required for a rail transit passenger.

Investing in Policies That Make Public Transportation Work

Public transportation systems in many areas are now beginning to experience their own congestion. Since 1995, public transportation ridership has grown over 22 percent—faster than both highway travel and airline travel—forcing many systems to the limits of their capacity, and sometimes beyond.

Substantial increases in public transportation investment are needed now to assure that current and planned services remain comfortable, convenient and attractive. To obtain the greatest return from that investment, however, renewed emphasis also must be placed on a number of existing, public transportation–supportive policies and initiatives.

> *"Expand[ing] the nation's public transit systems . . . will not notably reduce either existing or future peak-hour traffic congestion."*

Public Transportation Will Not Reduce Traffic Congestion

Anthony Downs

Traffic congestion is, and will continue to be, a fact of life in the United States, maintains Anthony Downs in the following viewpoint. In Downs's opinion, congestion is simply the result of economic prosperity. In addition, he says, congestion is a necessary consequence of Americans' desire to live in low-density settlements. For this reason, argues Downs, neither public transportation, nor any other proposals can reduce traffic congestion in America. Downs is a senior fellow at the Brookings Institution, a nonprofit public-policy research organization. He specializes in metropolitan policy.

As you read, consider the following questions:

1. What percentage of America's daily commuters use private vehicles, as cited by Downs?
2. According to the author, why does the theory of triple convergence mean that public transit cannot reduce congestion?

3. Why is public transit ineffective in low-density settlements, as argued by Downs?

Traffic congestion is not primarily a problem, but rather the solution to our basic mobility problem, which is that too many people want to move at the same times each day. Why? Because efficient operation of both the economy and school systems requires that people work, go to school, and even run errands during about the same hours so they can interact with each other. That basic requirement cannot be altered without crippling our economy and society. The same problem exists in every major metropolitan area in the world.

In the United States, the vast majority of people seeking to move during rush hours use private automotive vehicles, for two reasons. One is that most Americans reside in low-density areas that public transit cannot efficiently serve. The second is that privately owned vehicles are more comfortable, faster, more private, more convenient in trip timing, and more flexible for doing multiple tasks on one trip than almost any form of public transit. As household incomes rise around the world, more and more people shift from slower, less expensive modes of movement to privately owned cars and trucks.

With 87.9 percent of America's daily commuters using private vehicles, and millions wanting to move at the same times of day, America's basic problem is that its road system does not have the capacity to handle peak-hour loads without forcing many people to wait in line for that limited road space. Waiting in line is the definition of congestion, and the same condition is found in all growing major metropolitan regions. In fact, traffic congestion is worse in most other countries because American roads are so much better.

Coping with the Mobility Problem

There are four ways any region can try to cope with the mobility challenge. But three of them are politically impractical or physically and financially impossible in the United States.

Charging peak-hour tolls. Governments can charge people money to enter all the lanes on major commuting roads during peak hours. If tolls were set high enough and collected electronically with "smart cards," the number of vehicles on each major road during peak hours could be reduced enough so that vehicles could move at high speeds. That would allow more people to travel per lane per hour than under current, heavily congested conditions.

Transportation economists have long been proponents of this tactic, but most Americans reject this solution politically for two reasons. Tolls would favor wealthier or subsidized drivers and harm poor ones, so most Americans would resent them, partly because they believe they would be at a disadvantage.

The second drawback is that people think these tolls would be just another tax, forcing them to pay for something they have already paid for through gasoline taxes. For both these reasons, few politicians in our democracy—and so far, anywhere else in the world—advocate this tactic. Limited road-pricing schemes that have been adopted in Singapore, Norway, and London only affect congestion in crowded downtowns, which is not the kind of congestion on major arteries that most Americans experience.

Greatly expanding road capacity. The second approach would be to build enough road capacity to handle all drivers who want to travel in peak hours at the same time without delays. But this "cure" is totally impractical and prohibitively expensive. Governments would have to widen all major commuting roads by demolishing millions of buildings, cutting down trees, and turning most of every metropolitan region into a giant concrete slab. Those roads would then be grossly underutilized during non-peak hours. There are many occasions when adding more road capacity is a good idea, but no large region can afford to build enough to completely eliminate peak-hour congestion.

Greatly expanding public transit capacity. The third approach would be to expand public transit capacity enough to shift so many people from cars to transit that there would be no more excess demand for roads during peak hours. But in the United States in 2000, only 4.7 percent of all commuters traveled by public transit. (Outside of New York City, only 3.5 percent use transit and 89.3 percent use private vehicles.) A major reason is that most transit commuting is concentrated in a few large, densely settled regions with extensive fixed-rail transit systems. The nine U.S. metropolitan areas with the most daily transit commuters, when taken together, account for 61 percent of all U.S. transit commuting, though they contain only 17 percent of the total population. Within those regions, transit commuters are 17 percent of all commuters, but elsewhere, transit carries only 2.4 percent of all commuters, and less than one percent in many low-density regions.

Even if America's existing transit capacity were tripled and fully utilized, morning peak-hour transit travel would rise to 11.0 percent of all morning trips. But that would reduce all morning private vehicle trips by only 8.0 percent—certainly progress, but hardly enough to end congestion—and tripling public transit capacity would be extremely costly. There are many good reasons to expand the nation's public transit systems to aid mobility, but doing so will not notably reduce either existing or future peak-hour traffic congestion.

Living with congestion. This is the sole viable option. The only feasible way to accommodate excess demand for roads during peak periods is to have people wait in line. That means traffic congestion, which is an absolutely essential mechanism for American regions—and most other metropolitan regions throughout the world—to cope with excess demands for road space during peak hours each day.

Although congestion can seem intolerable, the alternatives would be even worse. Peak-hour congestion is the balancing mechanism that makes it possible for Americans to pursue other goals they value, including working or sending their children to school at the same time as their peers, living in low-density settlements, and having a wide choice of places to live and work.

The Principle of Triple Convergence

The least understood aspect of peak-hour traffic congestion is the principle of triple convergence.... This phenomenon occurs because traffic flows in any region's overall transportation networks form almost automatically self-adjusting relationships among different routes, times, and modes. For example, a major commuting expressway might be so heavily congested each morning that traffic crawls for at least thirty minutes. If that expressway's capacity were doubled overnight, the next day's traffic would flow rapidly because the same number of drivers would have twice as much road space. But soon word would spread that this particular highway was no longer congested. Drivers who had once used that road before and after the peak hour to avoid congestion would shift back into the peak period. Other drivers who had been using alternative routes would shift onto this more convenient expressway. Even some commuters who had been using the subway or trains would start driving on this road during peak periods. Within a short time, this triple convergence onto the expanded road during peak hours would make the road as congested as it was before its expansion.

Experience shows that if a road is part of a larger transportation network within a region, peak-hour congestion cannot be eliminated for long on a congested road by expanding that road's capacity.

The triple convergence principle does not mean that expanding a congested road's capacity has no benefits. After ex-

Gamble. © 1999 by *The Florida Times-Union.* Reproduced by permission.

pansion, the road can carry more vehicles per hour than before, no matter how congested it is, so more people can travel on it during those more desirable periods. Also, the periods of maximum congestion may be shorter, and congestion on alternative routes may be lower. Those are all benefits, but that road will still experience some period of maximum congestion daily.

Triple Convergence and Other Proposals

Triple convergence affects the practicality of other suggested remedies to traffic congestion. An example is staggered work hours. In theory, if a certain number of workers are able to commute during less crowded parts of the day, that will free up space on formerly congested roads. But once traffic moves faster on those roads during peak hours, that will attract other drivers from other routes, other times, and other modes where conditions have not changed to shift onto the improved roads.

161

Soon the removal of the staggered-working-hour drivers will be fully offset by convergence.

The same thing will happen if more workers become telecommuters and work at home, or if public transit capacity is expanded on off-road routes that parallel a congested expressway. This is why building light rail systems or even new subways rarely reduces peak-hour traffic congestion. In Portland, where the light rail system doubled in size in the 1990s, and in Dallas, where a new light rail system opened, congestion did not decline for long after these systems were up and running. . . .

Low-Density Settlements

Another crucial factor contributing to traffic congestion is the desire of most Americans to live in low-density settlements. In 1999, the National Association of Homebuilders asked 2,000 randomly-selected households whether they would rather buy a $150,000 townhouse in an urban setting that was close to public transportation, work, and shopping or a larger, detached single-family home in an outlying suburban area, where distances to work, public transportation, and shopping were longer. Eighty-three percent of respondents chose the larger, farther-out suburban home. At the same time, new workplaces have been spreading out in low-density areas in most metropolitan regions.

Past studies, including one published in 1977 by Boris S. Pushkarev and Jeffery M. Zupan, have shown that public transit works best where gross residential densities are above 4,200 persons per square mile; relatively dense housing is clustered close to transit stations or stops; and large numbers of jobs are concentrated in relatively compact business districts.

But in 2000, at least two thirds of all residents of U.S. urbanized areas lived in settlements with densities of under 4,000 persons per square mile. Those densities are too low for public transit to be effective. Hence their residents are compelled to rely on private vehicles for almost all of their travel, including trips during peak hours.

Recognizing this situation, many opponents of "sprawl" call for strong urban growth boundaries to constrain future growth into more compact, higher-density patterns, including greater reinvestment and increased densities in existing neighborhoods. But most residents of those neighborhoods vehemently oppose raising densities, and most American regions already have densities far too low to support much public transit. So this strategy would not reduce future traffic congestion much. . . .

Here to Stay

Peak-hour traffic congestion in almost all large and growing metropolitan regions around the world is here to stay. In fact, it is almost certain to get worse during at least the next few decades, mainly because of rising populations and wealth. This will be true no matter what public and private policies are adopted to combat congestion.

But this outcome should not be regarded as a mark of social failure or misguided policies. In fact, traffic congestion often results from economic prosperity and other types of success.

Although traffic congestion is inevitable, there are ways to slow the rate at which it intensifies. Several tactics could do that effectively, especially if used in concert, but nothing can eliminate peak-hour traffic congestion from large metropolitan regions here and around the world. Only serious economic recessions—which are hardly desirable—can even forestall an increase.

For the time being, the only relief for traffic-plagued commuters is a comfortable, air-conditioned vehicle with a well-equipped stereo system, a hands-free telephone, and a daily commute with someone they like.

Congestion has become part of commuters' daily leisure time, and it promises to stay that way.

| *"Increasing automobile fuel economy standards . . . would reduce the oil used by cars and trucks."*

Fuel Efficiency Standards Should Be Raised

Gretchen DuBeau

In this study Gretchen DuBeau, a global warming advocate at the U.S. Public Interest Research Group (U.S. PIRG) Education Fund, argues that the United States needs to raise its Corporate Average Fuel Economy (CAFE) standards—the laws that regulate fuel economy. According to the study, this would greatly reduce oil use by cars and trucks. As a result, DuBeau maintains, Americans would save billions of dollars every year and would be less dependent on foreign oil supplies. The Education Fund is the research and education center for U.S. PIRG, a public interest group that uses investigative research, grassroots organizing, advocacy, and litigation to fight threats to public health and well-being in the United States.

As you read, consider the following questions:

1. Why do automakers often add weight to their trucks, as argued by the author?
2. According to the author, how many barrels of oil could be saved every day by 2020 if fuel economy

Gretchen DuBeau, "Going Nowhere: The Price Consumers Pay for Stalled Fuel Economy Policies," *U.S. PIRG Education Fund*, May 2004. Copyright © 2004 by the U.S. PIRG Education Fund. Reproduced by permission.

standards were increased to 40 miles per gallon?

3. How much of U.S. domestic petroleum consumption is used for transportation, according to the author?

In response to the Arab oil embargo of the early 1970s, Congress implemented the first miles per gallon standards in 1975 to protect consumers from high gasoline prices and supply vulnerability resulting from U.S. dependence on foreign oil. The drafters of the successful oil savings law recognized that the only way to reduce dependence on foreign oil was to reduce oil demand, requiring cars and light trucks to increase miles per gallon averages to 27.5 and 20.7 miles, respectively. As a result, consumers were able to go farther on a gallon of gas; these standards also had the benefit of reducing tailpipe emissions, including emissions of global warming gases.

A Record Low for Fuel Standards

Today [2004], average fuel economy is at a 23-year low of 20.8 mpg for model year 2003 light cars and trucks—six percent lower than the peak value of 22.1 mpg achieved in 1987 and 1988. The general overall declining trend in new light-vehicle fuel economy is due to the recent light truck and SUV [sport utility vehicle] boom. "Light trucks" (minivans, pickups, and SUVs) are defined as weighing less than 8,500 pounds. Because fuel economy standards separate light trucks as a class and subject them to different fuel economy standards, automakers often add weight to their trucks to exempt them from the miles per gallon standards altogether. Trucks weighing 8,600 pounds or more, such as the Hummer, Suburban, Tahoe, and Excursion, fall through this loophole and get significantly lower miles per gallon than even the light trucks. The Suburban, for example, gets between 10 and 18 miles per gallon, and the Tahoe gets between 14 and 18.

One reason SUVs are so popular is the auto industry's advertising campaign to convince the American people that

SUVs, because of their weight, are safer than smaller automobiles. However, according to the Alliance of Automobile Manufacturers, SUV occupants are 3.5 percent more likely to die in crashes than sedan occupants. Most SUVs have a much narrower and taller profile with a higher center of gravity, making them more prone to rollover in a blowout or when the driver takes a corner too fast. . . .

Increasing Fuel Economy

In 2001, NAS [National Academy of Sciences] identified ranges of fuel economy improvements for both cars and trucks while holding acceleration, performance, size, accessories, amenities, the mix of vehicle types, makes, and models sold constant. The result was a 2002 NAS report, *Effectiveness and Impact of Corporate Average Fuel Economy (CAFE) Standards*, which concluded that automakers could use existing technology to increase the fuel economy of their fleets to 40 mpg over the next decade while improving safety and maintaining performance.

According to the Union of Concerned Scientists, increasing automobile fuel economy standards to 40 mpg over a ten-year period would:

- Reduce the oil used by cars and trucks by one-third in 2020;

- Save four million barrels of oil each day by 2020 (this is 10 times the projected daily yield from the Arctic National Wildlife Refuge in the same year);

- Save consumers $16 billion at the gas pump; and

- Cut global warming emissions from vehicles by 20 percent.

The technology is available today to make cars and light trucks go farther on a gallon of gas. The Toyota Prius, which gets 55 estimated combined miles per gallon, and the Ford

SUV Escape, which gets 35–40 mpg, demonstrate that foreign and domestic manufacturers can produce smarter engines, more efficient transmissions, and other design improvements to make substantial gains in fuel economy. . . .

The auto industry has long opposed any meaningful increase in fuel economy standards, even during times of high gas prices. The Bush administration has failed to act to apply our technological know-how to improve the fuel economy of America's cars, which has led to higher prices at the pump, increased dependence on foreign oil, and a host of environmental problems stemming from oil exploration and combustion. In fact, the Bush administration has actively opposed proposals to significantly increase the fuel economy of cars and light trucks. . . .

Paying More at the Gas Pump

About 30.9 million Americans are expected to travel 50 miles or more from home by car this Memorial Day weekend [2004] for a total of 1.5 billion miles. With gasoline priced at $2.02 per gallon on average and even higher in some parts of the country, the three-day excursions will cost consumers approximately $150 million. If automobile fuel economy standards were at 40 mpg instead of a fleetwide 20.8 mpg, the holiday trips would only cost consumers $78 million. Americans will pay $72 million more than necessary for gasoline to drive to their vacation destinations this Memorial Day weekend.

The best way to protect consumers from high gasoline prices is to reduce demand by increasing miles per gallon standards to 40 mpg. Consumers would be able to travel almost twice as far before filling up their tanks and would save $72 million over the three-day Memorial Day weekend alone.

Oil use for transportation in the U.S. accounts for more than two-thirds of domestic petroleum consumption—67.1 percent, which is 150 percent of domestic production. This

A Matter of Priority and Will

Government and industry have made great strides in developing technologies that can improve the fuel efficiency of the transportation sector (e.g, lightweight materials, variable valve transmissions, electric motors and controllers, low rolling resistance tires, etc.). Many of these technologies are not, however, being widely used to improve the fuel economy of today's vehicle fleet; instead, they are being used to increase overall vehicle acceleration, power and size. Without government policy intervention, the next 20 years could be just like the last, with fuel economy being sacrificed to increased acceleration, horsepower, weight and size.

By wisely using the tax code and increasing and reforming [Corporate Average Fuel Economy] standards, we could begin to see improvements in the fuel economy of vehicles. Despite the arguments of the auto industry, these policies would not deny consumer choice. These policies would simply change the relative price of various vehicle amenities. They would make increased fuel economy *less* expensive. They would make hot rods and large tow vehicles more expensive. They would make people think about how much car or truck they really need. They would encourage manufacturers to make more vehicles with better fuel economy available to consumers, and then market them.

In sum, improving fuel economy is not a technical challenge—the technologies are here. Rather it is a matter of political priority and will.

Joe Loper, congressional testimony, July 28, 2005.

means that our infatuation with the automobile alone consumes more oil than the United States can produce. In 2002, the U.S. imported 53 percent of the nation's oil—11.53 million barrels of oil, but consumed 21.84 million barrels of oil.

This Memorial Day [2004], Americans will use 35.7 million more gallons of gas than they would under a 40 mpg fuel economy standard. The increased gasoline usage equates to 1.8 million more barrels of oil that will have to be imported from abroad.

Too Dependent on Oil

America is simply too dependent on oil. The United States holds only two percent of the world's oil reserves. It produces 10.4 percent of the world's petroleum but consumes 25.5 percent of the world's total petroleum production. Our heavy reliance on oil products to fuel transportation vehicles takes a heavy toll on the environment. Oil and gas pollute the environment from the point of extraction to combustion, leaving a trail of oil spills, smog-forming air pollution, and global warming.

Despite the environmental, consumer, and economic problems with oil dependence, the Bush administration has supported efforts by Congress to enact an energy policy that would actually increase U.S. oil consumption by adding new loopholes to current automobile fuel economy standards. According to a recent analysis by the Energy Information Administration (EIA), by 2025, U.S. imports of petroleum would have increased by 82.9 percent under the administration's preferred energy policy, only slightly less than business as usual. . . .

Failure to Act

Increasing automobile fuel economy standards to 40 miles per gallon would reduce the oil used by cars and trucks by one-third in 2020 and save consumers $16 billion at the gas pump. Unfortunately, the federal government has not enacted a meaningful increase in fuel economy in almost 30 years.

> "[CAFE] constrains the production of larger cars. And in most modes of collision, larger, heavier cars are more protective of their occupants."

Fuel Efficiency Standards Harm Americans

Sam Kazman

In the following viewpoint Sam Kazman maintains that America's Corporate Average Fuel Economy (CAFE) standards—which regulate vehicle fuel economy—are harmful to Americans. These standards force car manufacturers to build smaller, lighter cars, explains Kazman. He believes these cars are less safe for their occupants in collisions. Kazman argues that the public has been falsely led to believe that CAFE standards are good for America while in reality they cause many deaths. Kazman is general counsel for the Competitive Enterprise Institute, a free-market advocacy organization in Washington, D.C. His writing has appeared in numerous publications, including the Washington Post, *the* Wall Street Journal, USA Today, *and* Regulation.

As you read, consider the following questions:

1. As explained by Kazman, what is the effect of larger mass in a multicar collision between cars of identical size?

Sam Kazman, "CAFE Standards: Do They Work? Do They Kill?" speech at the Heritage Foundation, February 25, 2002. Copyright © 2002 by the Competitive Enterprise Institute. Reproduced by permission.

2. According to the author, why is the improving death rate in cars unrelated to CAFE standards?

3. What does the insurance industry say about car size and safety, as argued by Kazman?

W hy does CAFE [Corporate Average Fuel Economy][1] kill? It does so because it constrains the production of larger cars. And in most modes of collision, larger, heavier cars are more protective of their occupants than are small cars. Let's consider first of all single vehicle crashes, where about fifty percent of all occupant deaths occur. Extra mass in a car involved in a collision with a tree, or a bridge abutment, or a brick wall, is incredibly protective. You find differences in survival rates between sub-compacts and larger cars on the order of four times as great or eight times as great. There is simply no question that in single vehicle crashes, larger, heavier cars are safer.

The other half of all occupant deaths, however, occur in multi-car collisions, largely in two-car collisions. And there, the issue gets a little more complicated. The analysis I'm about to give you is based on the work of Dr. Leonard Evans, who is head of the International Traffic Medicine Association, who's been a researcher in this field for three decades, and who has this up on his website at scienceservingsociety.com.

Car Mass and Safety

Essentially it's a very complex issue, but the net effects tend to be very small. In multi-car collisions, adding mass to your car protects you more, but it does put the occupants of the other car at somewhat greater risk. And so the question is: what is the net effect? Does society benefit—or is it hurt—by adding mass to the car that you're driving?

1. These standards, first enacted in 1975, regulate fuel economy of vehicles in the United States. One way to meet CAFE standards is to manufacture a smaller, lighter vehicle.

Here's how it breaks down. When the two cars that are involved in that multi-car collision are pretty much identical, larger mass helps the occupants of both cars. When they're not identical, but they're pretty similar to each other, adding mass to your car tends to protect you and it hurts the occupants of the other car. But its net effect is protective, and so society benefits there as well from added mass.

Finally, when there's a huge difference between the mass of your car and the car you strike, the extra mass in your car actually poses a disservice to society. That is, it adds more risk for the people in the other car than it does to protect you.

When you add all of those scenarios together, in the area of multi-car collisions, it's not clear what the answer is. But it is a relatively small effect. In Dr. Evans' view, added mass in multi-car collisions probably benefits society. In the view of some other people, it hurts overall social safety. But whatever that multi-car effect of mass is, it's totally outweighed by the protection offered by added mass in single car collisions. And for that reason, in Dr. Evans' words, "CAFE kills. More stringent CAFE standards will kill even more."

Some people ask about the National Highway Traffic Safety Administration's tests? NHTSA has multi-star test ratings for cars, based on crashing them into nondeformable barriers. We see small cars getting three and four stars—top ratings from NHTSA—and we also see large cars getting three and four stars. So small cars seem to do as well as large cars here.

Well, the problem is that if you look at the NHTSA test results, they expressly state that you cannot compare these ratings across different weight classes. In fact, NHTSA's test results also used to say—before they went on the web—that larger cars are more protective than small cars. I can't find that statement on the web, and that's something I'll get back to—how the political incorrectness of large cars has incredibly distorted the information that we're getting.

The Technology Argument

Now, what arguments do proponents of CAFE—especially those who want to make CAFE more stringent—offer? They essentially offer three arguments and one image, and let me quickly describe them.

The first argument is that new technology can get us out of this bind. It can give us much higher fuel economy *and* much greater safety, and so there is no tradeoff here. Now I want you, as a thought experiment, to imagine the most high tech car you can. It's got incredibly advanced, incredibly efficient valves and engines, and incredibly great safety devices. Picture that car in your mind, and then add a few additional cubic feet to that car and a few additional pounds, to make it a little bit bigger, and a little heavier.

Two things happen. This high tech car, once you made it bigger, is a bit safer. But it's also a bit less fuel-efficient. That is, you've got a tradeoff even at this incredibly high tech frontier. You've got a tradeoff between safety and fuel economy.

And so high technology doesn't get you out of this bind. As Leonard Evans says, this is like a tobacco industry executive saying that smoking doesn't endanger your health, because with everything we now know about eating right and exercising right, you can smoke and still be as healthy as a non-smoker.

Well, it's true that, with what we know about diet and exercise, smokers can be healthier. But this knowledge can make a *non* smoker even healthier yet. And if you smoke, you're going to be taking a risk.

The folks who are selling you CAFE, more stringent CAFE, on the basis of high technology, are arguing with no different logic than that. It's as if they were trying to sell you tobacco with the claim that it's risk-free. There *is* a risk, no matter what technologies are developed.

Fake Interpretation of Death Rate Decline

What is the second argument? It's this: . . . We see that since the 1970's, when CAFE was enacted, [the death rate in cars] has steadily improved. And yet, cars have been downsized. The average car today is 900 to 1,000 pounds lighter than it was in the mid 1970's. How can you tell me that downsizing cars makes them more dangerous when the death rate has been steadily improving?

To answer that, let me do an analogy. I'm going to use that same logic to show you that AIDS is not a health threat. Because in 1970 we had zero cases of AIDS. Now, we've got several tens of thousands. And yet longevity—life expectancy—in the U.S. now, is about ten months greater than it was in 1970. So how can you tell me that AIDS is a health threat when longevity has been improving?

Well, the real answer is that longevity has been improving not just since AIDS appeared, but since it began to be recorded. Human life expectancy has been steadily getting better. Were it not for AIDS, it would be even better still. The same is true for the death rate in cars. It has been improving, not just since we began to downsize cars, but since we began to actually record the data. And it would have improved even more.

You cannot look at a long-term improving trend in traffic safety and use it to argue against the effects of CAFE.

Politically Incorrect

What's the last argument they use? They say: CAFE can't be deadly. It's endorsed by [political activist] Ralph Nader, [former head of NHTSA] Joan Claybrook, and [executive director of the Center for Auto Safety] Clarence Ditlow. This is exactly what they say. If you go to the Sierra Club's web page on global warming and CAFE, and go to the questions and answers, the very first question asks, doesn't CAFE undermine safety? The very first answer is: Nonsense. . . .

Not Working

A closer look at CAFE reveals that it has failed to live up to any of its promises:

- CAFE hasn't improved energy independence. Fuel efficiency of cars on the road has climbed 52 percent since 1975, but that hasn't cut the nation's reliance on imported oil. Quite the opposite, in fact. Overall, the nation imports 51 percent of its oil, up from 36 percent in 1975. . . .

- CAFE has cost thousands of lives. [A National Research Council] report estimates that CAFE standards killed as many as 2,600 people in 1993 alone, thanks to the fact that the tighter fuel standards pushed automakers to downsize their fleets, forcing car buyers into smaller, less-safe cars than they would have otherwise purchased. In 1999, *USA Today* reported that CAFE had killed a total of 46,000 since the law was passed. That's equal, the story noted, to "roughly 7,700 deaths for every mile per gallon gained."

John Merline, Tech Central Station, February 12, 2003. www2. techcentralstation.com.

But long before large cars become so politically incorrect, these very same folks stated very forthrightly that larger cars are safer cars. In 1989, in a magazine interview, Ralph Nader was asked for advice on buying safer cars. He said, first, buy one with an airbag. Secondly, buy a larger car.

In 1972, Nader and Ditlow published a book called *Small on Safety*, a critique of the Volkswagen Beetle. Page after page in here has statements like: "Small size and light weight impose inherent limitations on the degree of safety that can be built into a vehicle."

What's happened? Back then, large cars were not politically incorrect. Now they are.

A month ago [January 2002], Joan Claybrook appeared before the Senate Commerce Committee, and gave a huge diatribe on how the CAFE-safety tradeoff was a myth propagated by industry. But in 1977, she appeared before that same committee and she said "There are going to be tradeoffs." The exact opposite.

Why have these folks taken this view on this position? Because for them, the line all along has been: You want more safety? You need more government. You need another government regulation if you want a safer product.

With CAFE, all of a sudden, it's exactly the opposite.

One other point here on the political incorrectness of large cars, and what's it meant for the information that consumers get: Every year *Consumer Reports* has an annual buying-guide issue. It comes out in April. It rates all the models. It has a very extensive discussion of how to buy a safer car.

You have to dig through that safety article, midway through or longer, to find any mention of the fact that larger cars are safer. In some years, it's not said at all.

On the other hand, go to the website of the industry that probably has the most direct stake in accurately assessing vehicle crashworthiness: the auto insurance industry. Go to the website of the Insurance Institute for Highway Safety [IIHS]. Look in their "Tips for Buying a Safer Car." One of the very first factors they mention is that large cars are safer than small cars.

You don't find it in *Consumer Reports*, but you do find it at the IIHS website.

CAFE Kills

Now, I said that proponents of CAFE have three arguments, and one image. What's the image? It's the image of a Ford Ex-

plorer devastating a Geo Metro. A large SUV [sport utility ve-
hicle] just killing everyone inside a sub-compact when there's
a collision between the two. It's a very gripping image, but it's
very, very unrepresentative of the total universe of vehicle collisions. According to the Insurance Institute, it is a highly ir-
representative example. And the real issue isn't so much the
larger size of the Explorer, but the small size of that sub-
compact. If you want to improve auto safety, you have to do
something about the size of the sub-compacts.

And, by the way, suppose you do use CAFE to start shrink-
ing the size of the Explorer. Well, look at the fatality data, the
rollover data for SUVs alone; it turns out that smaller SUVs
are much less safe than larger ones. Just as with passenger
cars. . . .

No one pushing for higher CAFE admits that it kills anyone. One thing that they claim is that, with higher CAFE, we
would be kept out of all of these blood-for-oil wars.[2]

But in a sense, CAFE itself is a blood-for-oil battle. And it
is waged not with knowing soldiers—with a military that
knows it's being put at risk—but with civilians who have no
idea that they're being placed in any danger whatsoever.

2. Some people argue that the United States becomes involved in foreign conflicts in order to ensure a steady oil supply.

| *"If biofuels take off, they will cause a global humanitarian disaster."*

The Use of Biofuels Will Harm Society

George Monbiot

The widespread use of biofuels will cause both environmental destruction and a humanitarian disaster, maintains George Monbiot in the following viewpoint. According to Monbiot, if the world turns to biofuels as an alternative to gasoline, arable land will be used to produce these fuels rather than food, and many of the world's poor will starve. In addition, he argues, the large-scale agriculture required to produce biofuels will be environmentally destructive. Monbiot writes a weekly column for the Guardian *newspaper. In 1995 he received the United Nations' Global 500 Award for outstanding environmental achievement.*

As you read, consider the following questions:

1. Why are biofuels being promoted as a solution to global climate change, as explained by the author?
2. According to Monbiot, while 800 million people are permanently malnourished, what has happened to the number of livestock on earth since 1950?
3. How has the production of biofuels affected Brazil's *cerrado*, as explained by the author?

If human beings were without sin, we would still live in an imperfect world. [Economist] Adam Smith's notion that by pursuing his own interest, a man "frequently promotes that of ... society more effectually than when he really intends to promote it", and Karl Marx's picture of a society in which "the free development of each is the condition for the free development of all" are both mocked by one obvious constraint. The world is finite. This means that when one group of people pursues its own interests, it damages the interests of others.

Embracing Biofuels

It is hard to think of a better example than the current enthusiasm for biofuels. These are made from plant oils or crop wastes or wood, and can be used to run cars and buses and lorries. Burning them simply returns to the atmosphere the carbon that the plants extracted while they were growing. So switching from fossil fuels to biodiesel and bioalcohol is now being promoted as the solution to climate change....

Everyone seems happy about this. The farmers and the chemicals industry can develop new markets, the government can meet its commitments to cut carbon emissions, and environmentalists can celebrate the fact that plant fuels reduce local pollution as well as global warming. Unlike hydrogen fuel cells, biofuels can be deployed straightaway. This, in fact, was how Rudolf Diesel expected his invention to be used. When he demonstrated his engine at the World Exhibition in 1900, he ran it on peanut oil. "The use of vegetable oils for engine fuels may seem insignificant today", he predicted. "But such oils may become in course of time as important as petroleum." Some enthusiasts are predicting that if fossil fuel prices continue to rise, he will soon be proved right.

I hope not. Those who have been promoting these fuels are well-intentioned, but wrong. They are wrong because the world is finite. If biofuels take off, they will cause a global humanitarian disaster....

A Renewable Source of Energy

Is biodiesel renewable? Any resource is renewable only if it is extracted at a rate no greater than it is replenished. Overcutting a forest or overfishing a fishery renders a renewable resource nonrenewable. Given that biodiesel potentially involves taking human food from the top of the ecological pyramid and feeding it to automobiles, the renewability issue is paramount.

Most people do not spend a lot of time sitting around thinking about the global food supply, but if we are going to feed human food to cars, we have to ask that question. We get our food from a number of sources. Do you know when the world fish catch peaked? In the early 1980s. What about grain production? Per capita production peaked in 1993. A lion's share of human food is grown on irrigated land. How is the supply of irrigated land holding up? Because of salinization, erosion, and other management issues, the per-capita global supply of irrigated farm land has shrunk considerably in the last several decades. The final humbling fact is that, even though the U.S. has the most productive agricultural system in the world, we are now a nation that teeters on the brink of agricultural debtorship.

Alexis, October 15, 2004. http://cvilleindymedia.org.

Impact on the Food Supply

The impact on global food supply will be catastrophic: big enough to tip the global balance from net surplus to net deficit. If, as some environmentalists demand, it is to happen worldwide, then most of the arable surface of the planet will be deployed to produce food for cars, not people.

This prospect sounds, at first, ridiculous. Surely if there were unmet demand for food, the market would ensure that crops were used to feed people rather than vehicles? There is no basis for this assumption. The market responds to money, not need. People who own cars have more money than people at risk of starvation. In a contest between their demand for fuel and poor people's demand for food, the car-owners win every time. Something very much like this is happening already. Though 800 million people are permanently malnourished, the global increase in crop production is being used to feed animals: the number of livestock on earth has quintupled since 1950. The reason is that those who buy meat and dairy products have more purchasing power than those who buy only subsistence crops.

Environmental Impact

Green fuel is not just a humanitarian disaster; it is also an environmental disaster. Those who worry about the scale and intensity of today's agriculture should consider what farming will look like when it is run by the oil industry. Moreover, if we try to develop a market for rapeseed biodiesel . . ., it will immediately develop into a market for palm oil and soya oil. Oilpalm can produce four times as much biodiesel per hectare as rape, and it is grown in places where labour is cheap. Planting it is already one of the world's major causes of tropical forest destruction. Soya has a lower oil yield than rape, but the oil is a by-product of the manufacture of animal feed. A new market for it will stimulate an industry that has already destroyed most of Brazil's cerrado (one of the world's most biodiverse environments) and much of its rainforest.

It is shocking to see how narrow the focus of some environmentalists can be. At a meeting in Paris last month [October 2004], a group of scientists and greens studying abrupt climate change decided that [British prime minister] Tony Blair's two big ideas—tackling global warming and helping Africa—could both be met by turning Africa into a biofuel production zone. This strategy, according to its convenor, "provides a sustainable development path for the many African countries that can produce biofuels cheaply". I know the definition of sustainable development has been changing, but I wasn't aware that it now encompasses mass starvation and the eradication of tropical forests. Last year [2003], the British parliamentary committee on environment, food and rural affairs, which is supposed to specialise in joined-up thinking, examined every possible consequence of biofuel production—from rural incomes to skylark numbers—except the impact on food supply.

We need a solution to the global warming caused by cars, but this isn't it. If the production of biofuels is big enough to affect climate change, it will be big enough to cause global starvation.

> "[Hybrids offer] high fuel economy without compromise."

Gas-Electric Hybrids Can Help America Meet Its Transportation Needs

John Rockhold

Gasoline-electric hybrids are an efficient and reliable form of transportation, asserts John Rockhold in the following viewpoint. According to Rockhold, while hybrids are still more costly than conventional cars, they are worth the extra cost in the long term because they use far less gasoline. These cars are no more expensive to maintain and just as easy to drive as conventional cars, he adds. He predicts that sales of hybrids in the United States will continue to grow rapidly. Rockhold is a contributing writer to Mother Earth News, *a print and online magazine that offers news and information on environmentally friendly living.*

As you read, consider the following questions:

1. According to Yates, how much more do hybrids cost than conventional vehicles?

2. How long does a hybrid battery typically last, according to the author?

John Rockhold, "The Hybrid Revolution: Cool, Capable, and Fun to Drive, Hybrids Also Can Save You Thousands of Dollars in Gas," *Mother Earth News*, October/November 2005, pp. 38–42. Copyright © 2005 by Ogden Publications, Inc. All rights reserved. Reproduced by permission.

3. How can a driver improve fuel economy when driving his or her hybrid, as explained by Yates?

Six years after the release of the Honda Insight—the bullet-like two-seater that was the first gasoline/electric hybrid vehicle available in the United States—high fuel economy without compromise is here to stay. Praised by motorheads and environmentalists alike, hybrids represent the most exciting advancement in personal transportation since, well, the internal-combustion engine. Spearheaded by the Toyota Prius, hybrids' popularity surge shows that a rapidly growing number of people want to be on the cusp of the hybrid revolution. Furthermore, with skyrocketing gas prices and dwindling global oil supplies, hybrids are becoming an increasingly wise investment.

In 2004, more than 83,000 hybrids were sold. In just the first half of this year [2005], more than 90,000 were sold; final 2005 sales may eclipse 200,000. Right now, hybrids account for less than 1 percent of the automobiles sold in the United States. But given their growth rate and the dozens of new models that will be available in the next several years—Toyota alone plans to introduce 10 more hybrid models within the next seven years—hybrids will soon have a significant share of the auto market. Already there are more hybrids in more size categories than most thought possible when the Insight arrived. Meanwhile, sales of large sport utility vehicles and trucks are dwindling.

Worth the Cost

Car-buyers also are willing to pay extra for hybrids—anywhere from $1,000 to $10,000 more than conventional vehicles. . . . But with tax incentives for hybrids and the rising cost of gas, it's possible to make up the low end of that hybrid premium in about five years. For example, compare a conventional vehicle with the average U.S. fuel economy of 21 miles per gallon to a 46-mpg hybrid (the average of the Accord, Civic, Escape, Insight and Prius hybrids). Assume you pay $2.20 a gallon for gasoline, with that price rising 10 cents annually (a modest estimate; inflation alone will increase prices by at least 5 cents a year). After five years, you'll save $4,658 with a hybrid; after 10 years, $10,287. . . .

Still, the hybrid premium can be intimidating at first glance. In a survey conducted by the Polk Center for Automotive Studies, 61 percent of those polled said the extra cost would be a deterrent to buying a hybrid. But if we're willing to pay hundreds or thousands extra for options such as larger engines, four-wheel drive or leather seats, why not invest in a technology that will actually pay dividends for years to come?

"There are a lot of features that aren't worth the extra cost, but people pay for them because they want those features," says Terry Penney, technology manager for advanced vehicle technologies at the National Renewable Energy Laboratory (NREL). Penney and his team have worked to develop and improve hybrid systems since the early 1990s. "You have to take the longer view, the real cost of gas and the environmental consequences of pollution. People have recently seen how gas prices can be volatile. Oil is now about $60 a barrel—where's it going to stop?"

How Hybrids Work

At the heart of every hybrid is the tandem of an internal-combustion engine (powered by gasoline) and an electric motor (powered by batteries). In conventional vehicles, automakers size gas engines to provide enough power for peak acceleration, but that level of power isn't needed most of the time. The addition of an electric motor allows for a smaller gas engine that uses less fuel and can run more often at its peak efficiency:

In most hybrids, when the vehicle idles, the gas engine shuts off and the electric motor is the sole source of power.

The electric motor also powers the hybrid at low speeds and supplements the gas engine with extra oomph when the driver accelerates quickly.

To recharge their batteries, hybrids capture kinetic energy as the vehicle slows down, a process called regenerative braking. In conventional vehicles, this energy is lost as heat when brakes apply friction. But in hybrids, the electric motor helps slow the car and transfers some of the kinetic energy to the batteries, which store the power for future use. Hybrids' conventional brakes kick in when needed, such as with sudden stops. Because hybrids recharge themselves, there's no need to plug them into an electrical outlet overnight. . . .

Buying and Owning a Hybrid

A year ago, long waiting lists greeted those who wanted to buy just about any hybrid model. Some shoppers remained in limbo for six months or more. Demand was intense and supply was limited—looking for a hybrid became a year-round version of shopping for the hottest, hard-to-find toy of the Christmas season. Production of hybrids, though, is constantly increasing in an effort to keep up with demand. Although unsold hybrids are rare on dealers' lots—most are spoken for before they arrive—wait time is usually just a few weeks.

High demand also has driven up the price of hybrids. Odds are you won't successfully haggle dealers for a bargain—in high-demand areas, hybrids frequently sell for several thousand dollars more than their retail prices. Some used hybrids, especially recent years of the Prius, sell for as much or more as they cost when brand-new. That's at least a good sign for resale value—most new cars sharply decline in value as soon as they leave dealers' lots. To get the best deal on a hybrid, be patient and search high and low. . . .

Owning a hybrid should be a worry-free experience—don't believe naysayers who claim they come loaded with extra maintenance costs. Their regular maintenance needs are

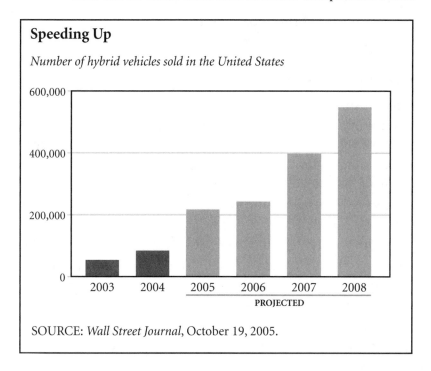

Speeding Up

Number of hybrid vehicles sold in the United States

PROJECTED

SOURCE: *Wall Street Journal*, October 19, 2005.

no different than gasoline-only vehicles, and the Honda Civic Hybrid and Toyota Prius have earned the highest ratings for reliability and owner satisfaction from *Consumer Reports*. In a now-famous quote within the hybrid community, Toyota mechanic Gus Heredia told the *Los Angeles Times*, "I'd go broke if the Prius was all I worked on."

Hybrids also are backed by the same warranties you'd expect with any new automobile. Additional warranties cover the hybrid systems and typically last for eight years or 100,000 miles. The hybrid components do not require any routine maintenance, and the batteries will work for about 200,000 miles or more. When they do expire, they can be recycled. . . .

In terms of safety, hybrids pose no more danger in a collision than any conventional vehicle. In fact, many hybrids offer the best in newer safety technologies, such as stability control, anti-lock brakes and side air bags. Here's more good news: given those safety features, you may even save money on insurance for a hybrid, especially if you're upgrading from an older vehicle and have a good driving record.

Driving a Hybrid

Initially, some hybrid owners find that their actual gas mileage doesn't live up to what's advertised. For many, the effort to improve their fuel economy becomes a diligent pursuit. Once drivers understand how hybrids work, they can adjust their driving habits to improve their mileage—for example, learning just when to press and release the accelerator to maximize coasting on the electric motor helps improve miles per gallon.

Consider, though, that the advertised fuel economy numbers may be slightly exaggerated. The Environmental Protection Agency (EPA) uses a 30-year-old methodology for calculating fuel economy. The tests do not account for modern influences on gas mileage such as air conditioning and speeds greater than 60 mph. The final numbers can be inflated by as much as 10 percent. . . .

Properly driven hybrids, though, will match their EPA-rated fuel economy more closely than nonhybrids, according to Amory Lovins, senior author of Winning the Oil Endgame and chief executive officer of Rocky Mountain Institute, an independent, nonprofit think tank devoted to energy and resource efficiency.

Lovins recommends pulse driving: "When you see that you'll need to slow or stop, start braking gently and as early as possible so you can recover the most braking energy for later use. If you brake too late—hence too hard the mechanical brakes will override, and they simply turn motion into useless heat."

Hybrids also are a justified excuse to accelerate with vigor. "Contrary to what we were taught in high school driver's education, when you're accelerating up to cruising speed, do so briskly," says Lovins, who owns a Honda Insight that gets 63 mpg. "The engine is most efficient at high speed and torque, so you'll use less fuel accelerating aggressively for a short time than accelerating slowly for a long time."

Also, take advantage of hybrids' computerized monitors that show which components are delivering power and report your fuel economy. "Consistent with attentive driving, keep an eye on the real-time mpg display and use the feedback to improve your driving habits," Lovins says.

Exactly how much your fuel economy will improve by driving a hybrid depends on numerous personal factors, but compared to gasoline vehicles, today's hybrids generally get 20 percent to 25 percent better fuel economy in highway driving, and 40 percent to 100 percent better mileage in city driving. Gas mileage in high-speed driving can improve if you avoid short trips and take a road with at least some hilly sections—the electric motor will kick in with steep inclines, aiding the gas engine's efficiency. For example, Penney—who drives a Prius—gets better results when he's on highways in Colorado's mountains than when driving through the city of Golden to reach the NREL office.

But stop-and-go driving does have the statistical edge. "It's generally true that stop-and-go driving is better [for hybrids' fuel economy] because you get regenerative braking, and that's always better than no regenerative braking." Penney says. "So if a hybrid is better for someone, it's for someone who does a lot of starting and stopping."

Translation: everyone. The bottom line is that driving a hybrid can be empowering—a personal, patriotic and environmental rush. The next time you spend $20 to $30 at the gas station, imagine not returning for another 500 miles.

> "[Hydrogen] fuel cell vehicles could pro-
> vide more than twice the efficiency of
> conventional vehicles."

Hydrogen-Powered Vehicles Can Help America Meet Its Transportation Needs

David K. Garman

*In the following viewpoint David K. Garman argues that by re-
placing gasoline-run automobiles with hydrogen-powered ones,
America can lessen its costly reliance on foreign oil and reduce
pollution. While such a transition will be difficult, he believes it
is necessary and can be achieved in the near future. Garman is
the undersecretary of energy for the U.S. Department of Energy.*

As you read, consider the following questions:

1. According to Garman, switching to hydrogen-powered
   vehicles would reduce auto emissions by what percentage?
2. How can the use of hydrogen-powered vehicles benefit the American economy, as argued by the author?
3. How many barrels of oil are required each day to fuel
   the nation's vehicles, according to Garman?

I n the early 1990s, the petroleum required just by our highway vehicles surpassed the amount produced domestically.

David K. Garman, testimony before the U.S. House Committee on Science, Washington, DC, March 5, 2003..

A Plentiful Fuel Source

The most common element in the universe, hydrogen has the highest energy content per unit weight of any known fuel. . . .

Once separated, hydrogen is the ultimate clean energy carrier. It can be non-polluting, is as safe as gasoline and can be produced anywhere.

NASA [National Aeronautics and Space Administration]'s space shuttles use hydrogen-powered fuel cells to operate electrical systems and the key emission, water, is consumed by the crew. . . .

It can be extracted from any substance with hydrogen: water, fossil fuels and even some organic matter.

FuelCellWorks, 2005. http://fuelcellworks.com.

The "gap" between production and transportation demand is growing—and is projected to keep growing. The current [2003] gap between total U.S. consumption and net production of oil is roughly 11 million barrels per day. Promoting efficiency in the use of oil, and finding new domestic sources of oil, are both important short-term undertakings. But over the long-term, a petroleum-free option is eventually required.

Our energy challenge is further complicated by another important factor—the pollutants and carbon dioxide emissions resulting from our use of energy. We have made tremendous progress in reducing pollutant emissions from our cars and trucks as well as our stationary power sources, and we will continue to make incremental gains. . . . But for true efficiency gains, we must reach to develop a wholly new approach to energy.

A Hydrogen-Based Future

In his [2003] State of the Union address, President Bush announced a groundbreaking plan to transform our Nation's energy future from one dependent on foreign petroleum, to one that utilizes the most abundant element in the universe—hydrogen.

Hydrogen can be produced from diverse domestic sources, freeing us from a reliance on foreign imports for the energy we use at home. Hydrogen can fuel ultra-clean internal combustion engines, which would reduce auto emissions by more than 99 percent. And when hydrogen is used to power fuel cell vehicles, it will do so with more than twice the efficiency of today's gasoline engines—and with none of the harmful air emissions. In fact, fuel cells' only by-products are pure water and some waste heat. . . .

Our current gasoline/hydrocarbon infrastructure has been forged in a competitive market. It is ubiquitous and remarkably efficient. It can deliver refined petroleum products that began as crude oil half a world away to your neighborhood for less than the cost of milk, drinking water, or many other liquid products you can buy at the supermarket. We are currently bound to that infrastructure. We have no alternative. Eventually replacing it with something different will be extremely difficult. But that is what we must do. . . .

The Benefits of Hydrogen

The Administration has committed to a large investment in hydrogen and fuel cells because it is convinced that the potential benefits of moving to a hydrogen economy are enormous. We can eventually eliminate our dependence on foreign energy sources. We can also maintain our transportation freedoms, the mobility that is so important to our quality of life and healthy economy. We can dramatically improve our air quality by eliminating polluting emissions from vehicles. Finally, hydrogen-powered vehicles can benefit our economy by reducing the financial drain associated with foreign energy purchases and by sustaining a strong international competitiveness in the transportation arena. . . .

Fueling Transportation

Every day, eight million barrels of oil are required to fuel the over 200 million vehicles that constitute our light duty transportation fleet. By 2025, the Nation's light vehicle energy consumption is projected to grow to as much as 14 million barrels per day of petroleum or its energy equivalent. Fuel cell vehicles could provide more than twice the efficiency of conventional vehicles . . . [resulting] in 11 million barrels per day savings by 2040 compared to what would otherwise be consumed in that year. . . .

A Commitment to Hydrogen

It will take a great deal to achieve this vision of a hydrogen energy future we are all talking about. . . . It will require careful planning and coordination, public education, technology development, and substantial public and private investments. It will require a broad political consensus and a bipartisan approach. Most of all, it will take leadership and resolve.

The President has demonstrated his leadership and resolve. "With a new national commitment," said the President during his State of the Union address, "our scientists and engineers will overcome obstacles to taking these cars from laboratory to showroom, so that the first car driven by a child born today could be powered by hydrogen and pollution free."

A few days later at an event on energy independence featuring new uses for fuel cells including automobiles, the President reiterated his commitment to his new Hydrogen Fuel Initiative stating, "The technology we have just seen is going to be seen on the roads of America. And it's important for our country to understand that by being bold and innovative, we can change the way we do business here in America; we can change our dependence upon foreign sources of energy; we can help with the quality of the air; and we can make a fundamental difference for the future of our children."

We believe that the benefits the President envisions are attainable within our lifetimes and will accrue to posterity, but they will require sustained work and investment of public and private financial resources. We at the Department of Energy welcome the challenge and opportunity to play a vital role in this Nation's energy future and to support our national security in such a fundamental way.

"*[The car] in your garage will be powered by a gasoline or diesel engine variant for the foreseeable future.*"

Gas and Diesel Engines Will Be the Mainstay of the Future

Brock Yates

In the following viewpoint Brock Yates points out that alternative-fuel vehicles have many flaws that restrict their use in the United States. While technologies such as the fuel cell and the electric car may seem promising, they will not replace gasoline or diesel engines anytime in the near future, he maintains. Moreover, while the gas-electric hybrid has been praised as an oil-saving alternative, says Brock, it is not a good solution to America's oil dependency because its operation requires oil. Yates is the author of Hot Rod: Resurrection of a Legend.

As you read, consider the following questions:

1. According to the author, what is the primary problem with the electric car?
2. While hydrogen is abundant in nature, what makes it difficult to use as an automobile fuel, according to Yates?
3. How have modern computer engine management systems improved gasoline engines, as explained by the author?

Brock Yates, "Segway to Nowhere," *American Spectator*, vol. 36, December 2003/ January 2004, pp. 58–59. Copyright © 2003 by *American Spectator*. Reproduced by permission.

B ad news for the car haters. Ms. Joan Claybrook, the nattering schoolmarm of Public Citizen, and Clarence Ditlow, the hand-wringer from the Center for Auto Safety and other shills for the Sierra Club and the Trial Lawyers of America, are in a funk. The most recent great white hope to run the gas-swilling, pollution-puffing, body-shredding, four-wheeled nightmare called the automobile off the American landscape has hit a ditch.

The Segway

You may recall the whoops of delight issuing from the elite media at last year's [2003] news that design guru Dean Kamen had solved the twenty-first century transportation problem with his invention of "Ginger," the code-name for his revolutionary two-wheeled miracle called the Segway.

It is a computer-controlled, all-electric "Human Transporter" that resembles a power lawnmower devoid of blades and a leaf bag. Thanks to Kamen's "Dynamic Stabilization" system the Segway is capable of toddling a rider at speeds up to 15 mph while a network of microchips and tiny motors keeps the device automatically in balance.

While the nation's news anchors and big-time print editors palpitated about the miracle machine, Kamen's Manchester, New Hampshire staff geared up for what they believed would be a boom in sales. Not only would granola-munchers abandon their hated automobiles in favor of Segways, but so would postal workers, warehouse operators, inner-city policemen, meter maids, and a veritable legion of Americans in all walks of life. The notion of a small, lightweight (well, relatively lightweight, at over 100 pounds) machine capable of behaving like a set of wheels attached to the ankles borders on the miraculous. Forget that its price tag is between $4,000 and $6,000 and that operating range is limited to 6–10 miles. Enthusiasts also choose to ignore the harsh reality that the Segway hates curbs, potholes and other simple obstructions. This has prompted several ugly tumbles, including one by an Atlanta police officer after he failed to navigate a downtown curb properly.

Worse yet, after several hours of operation, the Segway's batteries become sufficiently drained of power that its tiny computer brains gasp for juice. This prompts an involuntary retirement from duty, which in turn transforms the Segway into a loopy, Hal-like[1] renegade with little regard for its hapless rider. The miraculous "Dynamic Stabilization" having gone AWOL, the Segway "Human Transporter" becomes a runaway lawnmower on steroids, causing some ugly crashes.

Enter the saviors from the United States Consumer Products Safety Commission. After examining the issue, the solons of Washington stood by as Kamen and Co. issued a voluntary recall to install updated software that allegedly prevents such spills. The new system will provide proper warning before the volts take leave, thereby giving the rider time to scoot to the nearest 110-outlet for a re-charge. Once this is accomplished (warning: plan to wait an hour or more) the happy Segwayist is free to move about the country, presuming the landscape is flat, the weather is cooperative and infuriated pedestrians don't assault him as they leap out of the way.

Rather than a crazed rush to buy these magical devices celebrated by the ABTA (Anything But the Automobile), sales have been less than spectacular. The price tag has no doubt contributed to the limited volume of 6,000 units.

No matter, Kamen and his goofy scooter are still celebrated as a viable alternative to the hated car, which to the anointed is reviled at the same levels as toxic waste dumps and R. Emmett Tyrrell, Jr. commentaries. They of course choose to ignore the problems presented by, say, 100 million Segways plying the highways of the nation. Imagine the resulting overload on the wheezing power grid. This serves as another reminder

---

1. Hal is the fictional computer in the movie *2001: A Space Odyssey*, that eventually runs rampant.

Problems with Hydrogen

Hydrogen fuel cells have significant energy, economic, and environmental costs.

Hydrogen exists primarily bound in compounds like water. While seawater is plentiful, a substantial amount of energy is needed to separate its hydrogen and oxygen. Starting and ending with water as a supply of hydrogen means that fuel cells always use more energy than they provide.

The energy needed to get hydrogen by splitting it from water would come from the U.S. power supply. Thus, with fuel cell vehicles the dependence would be switched from petroleum to the power grid.

Decreasing vehicle petroleum use substantially by way of fuel cells would require great expansion of the U.S. electrical capacity, which is expected to grow 30 percent in the next 20 years in the absence of electrifying vehicles. At present, most U.S. electrical consumption is met by coal and natural gas, two fossil fuels that emit carbon dioxide.

Over the entire cycle of manufacturing and using hydrogen in fuel cell vehicles, more carbon dioxide would be emitted than for an efficient gasoline or diesel engine. Pollutants emitted from tailpipes would be lowered for fuel cell vehicles but would be displaced to electrical-generating facilities.

Sallie Baliunas, World & I, *November 2003.*

that for all the sensational ideas about alternative transportation devices like electric cars, fuel-cell vehicles, mass-transit trains and buses, etc., there is a smokestack at the point of origin.

Electric Cars and Fuel Cells

For example, while the electric car has been abandoned for a multitude of reasons—excessive weight, low performance, slow battery recharge time, expense, lead-acid, battery disposal issues—the primary cause was the realization that the national power grid could not supply sufficient juice for an electronic fleet sucking up the already limited energy supply. The fevered opposition by the Greenies (who of course advocate electrics) to build anything resembling more power plants, be they nuclear, hydro or coal-fired, added to the demise of the battery car.

Some fabulists now claim the fuel-cell is the hope of the future. Most automakers are hard at work on research to create these magical power sources that convert Hydrogen and Oxygen into electricity and a harmless exhaust of water droplets. Nirvana! Clean energy with no downside. But a few caveats remain. One: the expense and complexity of building, much less mass-producing, the polymer-electrolyte membrane that combines Hydrogen and Oxygen to generate electricity has not been solved. Two: Hydrogen, while abundant in nature, cannot be captured cheaply without massive power in puts. Its refinement, distribution and storage (remember the *Hindenburg*)[2] offer massive challenges that have not yet been solved. Therefore the possibility of the fuel-cell becoming a viable powerplant for normal, reasonably-priced automobiles lays far in the future, if ever—unless that revolutionary breakthrough in technology comes out of left field.

The Hybrid

In the short term the so-called hybrid engine—a simple combination of a conventional internal-combustion engine powering a small electrical generator that in turn propels the vehicle—seems viable. Both Honda and Toyota have efficient

2. In 1937 this hydrogen-filled zeppelin caught fire, killing thirty-six people.

hybrids (perhaps sold as loss-leaders) on the road, with every major automaker soon to follow.

Yet, for all the glories heaped on the hybrid as a saver of petroleum (about a 20 percent increase in fuel mileage in normal driving), one ugly truth haunts the Greenies. The primary power source for a Hybrid is the same old gasoline-powered engine of yore. Some units may employ high-efficiency diesels—providing certain stringent emission standards can be met—but the power source in the end is the same old Black Gold called Petroleum.

No Escape from Petroleum

Not only is it cheap (and probably to become even cheaper when the Iraq supply returns to normal volumes), but gasoline exists within a highly efficient production and distribution network. In the old days internal combustion engines were the filthy sources of carbon dioxide, nitrous-oxide, and carbon monoxide, but modern computer engine management systems and better designs have radically reduced the dangerous emissions to a point where some advance gasoline engines actually emit exhausts cleaner than the ambient air.

Trust me, for all the cheerleading by some politicians, lobbyists, environmentalist loonies and their handmaidens in the elite media, the old flivver in your garage will be powered by a gasoline or diesel engine variant for the foreseeable future. Save your money on a Segway and pass the tranquilizers to Ms. Claybrook and the Sierra Club.

Periodical Bibliography

The following articles have been selected to supplement the diverse views presented in this chapter.

Sallie Baliunas	"Economics of the Oil Alternatives," *World & I*, November 2003.
Thomas J. Davis	"Should Auto Fuel-Economy Standards Be Tightened to Reduce Dependence on Foreign Oil?" *CQ Researcher*, February 1, 2002.
Economist	"Stirrings in the Corn Fields—Biofuels," May 14, 2005.
Elizabeth Kolbert	"The Car of Tomorrow," *New Yorker*, August 11, 2003.
Hugo Martin	"7 Ways in Search of a Will," *Los Angeles Times Magazine*, August 29, 2004.
Katharine Mieszkowski	"Can Hydrogen Save Us?" *Yes!* Fall 2004.
New Republic	"Power Failure," July 4, 2005.
Michael Parfit	"Powering the Future," *National Geographic*, August 2005.
Alan Reynolds	"Redesigning Trucks," *Washington Times*, August 28, 2005.
John Rockhold	"The Hybrid Revolution: Cool, Capable, and Fun to Drive, Hybrids Also Can Save You Thousands of Dollars in Gas," *Mother Earth News*, October/November 2005.
John Semmens	"Does Light Rail Worsen Congestion and Air Quality?" *Ideas on Liberty*, June 2005.
Sacha Zimmerman	"Engines of Change," *Reader's Digest*, August 2005.

For Further Discussion

Chapter 1

1. Sam Kazman asserts that the car has liberated society while Jay Walljasper contends that automobiles restrict freedom. Based on your reading of these viewpoints, do you believe that car culture has given Americans freedom? Support your answer with examples from the viewpoints.

2. List three pieces of evidence that Barbara A. McCann and Reid Ewing use to support their argument that sprawl contributes to obesity. How might Wendell Cox and Ronald D. Utt view this support?

3. Three of the authors in Chapter 1 believe that cars have had a positive impact on American society while three authors believe the impact of cars has been negative. After reading this chapter, how do you think cars affect life in the United States? Cite from the texts to back up your position.

Chapter 2

1. Jeffrey W. Runge argues that the United States should enforce its seat belt laws. Ted Balaker contends that stricter laws would waste valuable government resources and violate personal freedom. In your opinion, should the government enforce seat belt laws? Why or why not?

2. List four pieces of evidence that Radley Balko offers to support his argument that America's drunk driving laws are too strict. Which do you think is strongest? Which is the weakest? Explain.

3. Amy Ridenour and Eric Peters maintain that in the event of an accident, an SUV offers its passengers more pro-

tection than does a typical passenger car. However, Joan Claybrook points out that the size of an SUV makes it unsafe to passenger cars on the road, which are easily crushed. Do you believe that the drivers of passenger cars need more protection against SUVs on the highways? Back up you answer by citing from the text.

4. Based on your reading of the viewpoints in Chapter 2, what do you believe would be the single most effective action America could take to increase the safety of its roads? Use examples and statistics from the viewpoints to support your argument.

Chapter 3

1. The *Denver Post* argues that teenagers under eighteen years old should never be allowed to participate in car racing, even if it is under supervision at a legal racetrack. How do you think Leonard Sax would respond to this opinion? Cite from the text to support your answer.

2. Wendy J. Hamilton argues that underage drunk driving rates are "inexcusably high," and she urges lawmakers to enhance efforts to stop teens from driving while intoxicated. Francine Katz contends that efforts to stop underage drunk driving are already successful, noting that there has been a significant decline in underage drunk driving rates. Hamilton is president of Mothers Against Drunk Driving while Katz is a vice president for brewing company Anheuser-Busch. How do their respective affiliations influence your evaluation of their arguments? Explain.

3. Melissa Savage argues that restrictions on youth driving will help decrease accident rates. The *Reno Gazette-Journal* maintains that driver education is one of the most important ways to help youths drive safely. Based on your reading of the viewpoints, which is the most effective way to increase the safety of youth driving? Why?

Chapter 4

1. The American Public Transportation Association and Anthony Downs discuss traffic congestion in the United States. On what points do they agree? On what points do they differ? Which author's viewpoint most strongly influences your views on the use of public transportation as a solution to congestion? Explain.

2. Fuel efficiency standards should be raised, according to Gretchen DuBeau. On the other hand, Sam Kazman maintains that fuel efficiency standards are harmful to Americans. Based on your reading of the viewpoints, which argument do you think is strongest? Why?

3. John Rockhold believes that gas-electric hybrids can help the United States meet its transportation needs while David K. Garman believes that hydrogen-powered vehicles are the answer. After reading these viewpoints, which do you believe is the most promising technology? Cite from the texts to support your answer.

4. The authors in Chapter 4 offer various opinions on how the United States can meet its transportation needs in the future. In your opinion, what is the most important change that the country needs to make in order to meet future transportation needs? Explain, citing from the viewpoints to support your answer.

Organizations to Contact

American Beverage Institute (ABI)
1775 Pennsylvania Ave. NW, Suite 1200
  Washington, DC 20006
(800) 843-8877
e-mail: abi@abionline.org
Web site: www.abionline.org

ABI is an association of restaurant operators that serve alcohol. The institute believes that antialcohol activists have gone too far in trying to restrict the consumption of adult beverages. It also believes that current blood alcohol concentration (BAC) limits are ineffective. The association publishes the *ABI Newsletter* along with numerous reports on the impact of BAC laws.

American Council for an Energy-Efficient Economy (ACEEE)
1001 Connecticut Ave. NW, Suite 801
  Washington, DC 20036
(202) 429-8873 • fax: (202) 429-2248
e-mail: info@aceee.org
Web site: www.aceee.org

ACEEE is a nonprofit organization that maintains that energy efficiency and conservation will benefit both the U.S. economy and the environment. The council publishes books and reports on ways to implement greater energy efficiency, including *Smart Energy Policies* and *Strategies for Reducing Oil Imports*.

American Petroleum Institute (API)
1220 L St. NW, Washington, DC 20005
(202) 682-8000
Web site: www.api.org

The American Petroleum Institute is a trade association representing America's petroleum industry. Its activities include lobbying, conducting research, and setting technical standards for the petroleum industry. API publishes numerous position papers on transportation-related issues, including papers calling for lower gasoline taxes and fewer restrictions on offshore drilling.

Brookings Institution
1775 Massachusetts Ave. NW
Washington, DC 20036
(202) 797-6000 • fax: (202) 797-6004
e-mail: brookinfo@brook.edu
Web site: www.brookings.org

The institution, founded in 1927, is a think tank that conducts research and education on numerous domestic issues including automobiles and transportation. Its publications include the quarterly *Brookings Review*, periodic *Policy Briefs*, and policy papers including "Auto-Mobility: Subsidizing America's Commute," and "Traffic Is Here to Stay."

Cato Institute
1000 Massachusetts Ave. NW
Washington, DC 20001
(202) 842-0200 • fax: (202) 842-3490
e-mail: cato@cato.org
Web site: www.cato.org

The Cato Institute is a libertarian public policy research foundation dedicated to limiting the role of government and promoting individual liberty. The institute publishes the quarterly magazine *Regulation*, the bimonthly *Cato Policy Report*, and numerous papers dealing with automobiles and transportation in the United States including "Let the Market Free Up Transportation in U.S." and "Leave Those SUVs Alone."

Council on Alternative Fuels (CAF)
1225 I St. NW, Suite 320
  Washington, DC 20005
(202) 898-0711

CAF is comprised of companies interested in the production of synthetic fuels and the research and development of synthetic fuels technology. It publishes information on new alternative fuels in the monthly *Alternative Fuel News.*

Heritage Foundation
214 Massachusetts Ave. NE
  Washington, DC 20002
(202) 546-4400 • fax: (202) 546-8328
Web site: www.heritage.org

The Heritage Foundation is a public policy think tank that advocates that the United States increase domestic oil production. Its publications include the quarterly magazine *Policy Review*, brief *Executive Memorandum* editorials, and the longer *Backgrounder* studies.

International Association for Hydrogen Energy (IAHE)
PO Box 248266, Coral Gables, FL 33124
(305) 284-4666
Web site: www.iahe.org

The IAHE is a group of scientists and engineers professionally involved in the production and use of hydrogen. It sponsors international forums to further its goal of creating an energy system based on hydrogen. The IAHE publishes the monthly *International Journal for Hydrogen Energy.*

National Commission Against Drunk Driving (NCADD)
1900 L St. NW, Suite 705
  Washington, DC 20036
(202) 452-6004 • fax: (202) 223-7012
e-mail: ncadd@trafficsafety.org
Web site: www.ncadd.com

NCADD comprises public and private sector leaders who are dedicated to minimizing the human and economic losses resulting from drunk-driving motor vehicle crashes. Working with private sector groups and federal, state, and local officials, NCADD develops strategies to target underage drinkers. The commission's publications include research abstracts, traffic safety facts, and the reports "The Dummy's Guide to Youth Alcohol Programs," and "Yes, You May Use the Car, but FIRST . . ."

National Highway Traffic Safety Administration (NHTSA)
400 Seventh St. SW, Washington, DC 20590
(888) 327-4236
Web site: www.nhtsa.dot.gov

The National Highway Traffic Safety Administration was established by the Highway Safety Act of 1970. It is responsible for reducing deaths, injuries, and economic losses resulting from motor vehicle crashes. This is accomplished by setting and enforcing safety performance standards for motor vehicles, and through grants to state and local governments to enable them to conduct effective local highway safety programs. NHTSA's Web site offers numerous reports, facts sheets, and links about automobiles and transportation in the United States.

National Resources Defense Council (NRDC)
40 W. 20th St., New York, NY 10011
(212) 727-2700
e-mail: nrdcinfo@nrdc.org
Web site: www.nrdc.org

The NRDC is a nonprofit activist group composed of scientists, lawyers, and citizens who work to promote environmentally safe energy sources and protection of the environment. NRDC publishes the quarterly magazine *OnEarth* and hundreds of reports, including "Cleaning Up Today's Dirty Diesels," "Is Hydrogen the Solution?" and "How Biofuels Can Help End America's Oil Dependence."

Reason Public Policy Institute (RPPI)

3415 S. Sepulveda Blvd., Suite 400
Los Angeles, CA 90034
(310) 391-2245 • fax: (310) 391-4395
e-mail: feedback@reason.org
Web site: www.rppi.org

RPPI is a research organization that supports less government interference in the lives of Americans. Their libertarian philosophy stands firmly opposed to raising the fuel economy standards of automobiles, arguing that doing so will necessitate smaller cars and thus result in more fatal traffic accidents. The institute publishes the monthly magazine *Reason.*

Renewable Fuels Association (RFA)

1 Massachusetts Ave. NW, Suite 820
Washington, DC 20001
(202) 289-3835 • fax: (202) 289-7519
e-mail: info@ethanolrfa.org
Web site: www.ethanolrfa.org

RFA is comprised of professionals who research, produce, and market renewable fuels, especially alcohol fuels. It also represents the renewable fuels industry before the federal government. RFA publishes the monthly newsletter *Ethanol Report.*

Sierra Club

85 Second St., Second Floor
San Francisco, CA 94105
(415) 977-5500 • fax: (415) 977-5799
e-mail: information@sierraclub.org
Web site: www.sierraclub.org

The Sierra Club is a grassroots organization with chapters in every state that promotes the protection and conservation of natural resources. The organization is opposed to sprawl and the increasing popularity of sport utility vehicles in the United States. It publishes the bimonthly magazine *Sierra* and the

Planet newsletter, which appears several times a year, and numerous reports including "Rail Transit in America," "A Time for Action," and "Increasing America's Fuel Economy."

Union of Concerned Scientists (UCS)
2 Brattle Square, Cambridge, MA 02238
(617) 547-5552 • fax: (617) 864-9405
e-mail: ucs@ucsusa.org
Web site: www.ucsusa.org

UCS is a nonprofit alliance of scientists who contend that energy alternatives to oil must be developed to reduce pollution and slow global warming. The union advocates raising the corporate average fuel economy (CAFE) standards with which automakers must comply, to forty miles per gallon by the year 2012. UCS publishes numerous articles and reports on alternative energy sources and ways to reduce fuel consumption, available on its Web site.

Bibliography of Books

Godfrey Boyle   *Renewable Energy.* New York: Oxford University Press, 2004.

Kenneth Deffeyes   *Hubbert's Peak: The Impending World Oil Shortage.* Princeton, NJ: Princeton University Press, 2003.

Kaitlen Jay Exum and Lynn M. Messina, eds.   *The Car and Its Future.* New York: H.W. Wilson, 2004.

Richard T.T. Forman   *Road Ecology: Science and Solutions.* Washington, DC: Island, 2003.

Mark S. Foster   *Nation on Wheels: The Automobile Culture in America Since 1945.* Belmont, CA: Wadsworth, 2003.

Howard Geller   *Energy Revolution: Policies for a Sustainable Future.* Washington, DC: Island, 2003.

Jonathan L. Gifford   *Flexible Urban Transportation.* New York: Pergamon, 2003.

David L. Goodstein   *Out of Gas: The End of the Age of Oil.* New York: W.W. Norton, 2004.

Owen D. Gutfreund   *Twentieth-Century Sprawl: Highways and the Reshaping of the American Landscape.* New York: Oxford University Press, 2004.

Gwendolyn Hallsmith   *The Key to Sustainable Cities: Meeting Human Needs, Transforming Community Systems.* Gabriola Island, Canada: New Society, 2003.

Jim Hinkley and
Jon G. Robertson

The Big Book of Car Culture: The Armchair Guide to Automotive Americana. Osceola, WI: Motorbooks International, 2005.

Peter W. Huber

The Bottomless Well: The Twilight of Fuel, the Virtue of Waste, and Why We Will Never Run Out of Energy. New York: Basic Books, 2005.

International
Energy Agency

Making Cars More Fuel Efficient: Technology for Real Improvements on the Road. Paris: OECD, 2005.

Michael T. Klare

Blood and Oil: The Dangers and Consequences of America's Growing Petroleum Dependency. New York: Metropolitan/Henry Holt, 2004.

Tom Kowalick

Fatal Exit: The Automotive Black Box Debate. Piscataway, NJ: Free Press, 2005.

Dom Nozzi

Road to Ruin: An Introduction to Sprawl and How to Cure It. Westport, CT: Praeger, 2003.

Adam L.
Penenberg

Tragic Indifference: One Man's Battle with the Auto Industry over the Dangers of SUVs. New York: HarperBusiness, 2003.

Jeremy Rifkin

The Hydrogen Economy: The Creation of the World-Wide Energy Web and the Redistribution of Power on Earth. New York: Jeremy P. Tarcher, 2002.

Paul Roberts — *The End of Oil: On the Edge of a Perilous New World*. New York: Houghton Mifflin, 2004.

Rudi Volti — *Cars and Culture: The Life Story of a Technology*. Westport, CT: Greenwood, 2004.

Michael H. Westbrook — *The Electric Car: Development and Future of Hybrid and Fuel-Cell Cars*. London: Institution of Electrical Engineers, 2001.

Peter Wollen and Joe Kerr, eds. — *Autopia: Cars and Culture*. London: Reaktion, 2002.

Index